Life

Life

A Critical User's Manual

Didier Fassin

polity

Excerpt from Samuel Beckett, *Waiting for Godot* copyright © 1954 by Grove Press, Inc.; Copyright © renewed 1982 by Samuel Beckett. Used in The United States and Canada by permission of Grove/Atlantic, Inc. Any third party use of this material, outside of this publication, is prohibited. Used in the World excluding the United States and Canada by permission of Faber and Faber Ltd.

First published in German as *Das Leben: Eine kritische Gebrauchsanweisung*, © Suhrkamp Verlag, Berlin, 2017

This English edition © Polity Press, 2018

Polity Press
65 Bridge Street
Cambridge CB2 1UR, UK

Polity Press
101 Station Landing
Suite 300
Medford, MA 02155, USA

ISBN-13: 978-1-5095-2664-2
ISBN-13: 978-1-5095-2665-9 (pb)

A catalogue record for this book is available from the British Library.

Library of Congress Cataloging-in-Publication Data
Names: Fassin, Didier, author.
Title: Life : a critical user's manual / Didier Fassin.
Other titles: Leben. English
Description: Cambridge, UK ; Medford, MA : Polity, 2018. | Translation of: Das Leben : eine kritische Gebrauchsanweisung. | Includes bibliographical references and index.
Identifiers: LCCN 2017048527 (print) | LCCN 2018005185 (ebook) | ISBN 9781509526680 (Epub) | ISBN 9781509526642 (hardback) | ISBN 9781509526659 (paperback)
Subjects: LCSH: Life. | BISAC: SOCIAL SCIENCE / Anthropology / Cultural.
Classification: LCC BD431 (ebook) | LCC BD431 .F2813 2018 (print) | DDC 113/.8–dc23
LC record available at https://lccn.loc.gov/2017048527

Typeset in 11 on 13 pt Sabon Roman by Toppan Best-set Premedia Limited
Printed and bound in the UK by CPI Group (UK) Ltd, Croydon, CR0 4YY

The publisher has used its best endeavours to ensure that the URLs for external websites referred to in this book are correct and active at the time of going to press. However, the publisher has no responsibility for the websites and can make no guarantee that a site will remain live or that the content is or will remain appropriate.

Every effort has been made to trace all copyright holders, but if any have been inadvertently overlooked the publisher will be pleased to include any necessary credits in any subsequent reprint or edition.

For further information on Polity, visit our website: politybooks.com

For Anne-Claire
in whose company
I have found it possible to envision
a user's manual for life

In isolation, a puzzle piece means nothing – just an impossible question, an opaque challenge. But as soon as you have succeeded in fitting it into one of its neighbors, the piece disappears, ceases to exist as a piece.... The two pieces so miraculously conjoined are henceforth one, which in its turn will be a source of error, hesitation, dismay, and expectation.

Georges Perec, *Life: A User's Manual*, 1987 [1978]

Contents

Acknowledgments

The honor conferred on me by the invitation to deliver the Adorno Lectures at the Institut für Sozialforschung at Goethe University, Frankfurt, is the only excuse I can offer to justify the ambitious project suggested by the title of this book. To tell the truth, it was not without some embarrassment that, in the months leading up to these lectures, my response to those who asked what my subject would be was that I would ponder about *life*. The apparent simplicity of a three-, four- or five-letter word (depending on whether it is uttered in French, English, or German) was undoubtedly deceptive, and my interlocutors' incredulous hesitance following this audacious yet enigmatic declaration forced me to give them something in the way of explanation. So I told them of my desire to think back through a series of primarily ethnographic studies I had undertaken over the last two decades on three continents, and to test a series of philosophical concepts that had both inspired me and left me unsatisfied through those years. I spoke of what had been a permanent quest, in all my various fieldworks, about ways of living and of treating human lives. I spoke of forms of life, of ethics of life, of politics of life. In short, in order to make sense of my empirical and theoretical questioning, I was attempting to provide them with a *user's manual*.

In part a form of homage to Georges Perec, who declared that "to live is to pass from one space to another, while doing your very best not to bump yourself," my use of this expression in the title of this book is also a way of bringing my project down to a more modest scale, making it more easily graspable, giving it the appearance of a bricolage, inviting readers to see it as a puzzle to be pieced together as they read. For all that, the subject of this text is indeed as the title states: it deals with life – and with lives. It would be easy, and certainly on one level true, to state that this is the guiding principle of a career that began in medicine and then diverted to anthropology: in turning from the teachings of biology to the gathering of biographies, I have moved from the life of organs to the life of human beings. But there is more to it than the fortunes of a professional trajectory. For my way of scrutinizing life through forms of life, ethics of life, and politics of life is not neutral. It is marked by the theme of inequality – the inequality of lives which, from my childhood in a public housing project to my discovery of non-Western societies through the extreme poverty I encountered in Indian cities, has formed my worldview. In fact this book could, perhaps more explicitly, have been titled "On the inequality of lives." If all of Perec's work is haunted by an absence – that of his parents, who died in World War II – I would say that my research is inhabited throughout by an awareness: that of unequal lives. Hence the addition of the adjective *critical* qualifying my user's manual for life.

In reworking these lectures for publication, I have felt it important to retain not only their progression – a triptych in which each part opens with a theoretical exposition that serves as an introduction to the empirical investigation, with the aim of proposing a new synthesis – but also the context – the reference to Adorno at the beginning of the book, and the reminder, in the epilogue to each chapter, of the tragic events that accompanied the elaboration of *Minima Moralia*. All writing has a history. I wanted to preserve the spirit of these lectures, given in Frankfurt at the institution where one of the most important forms of social critique was born nearly a century ago, and has continued to be practiced and developed since that time. This of course gives me the opportunity to express my gratitude to Axel Honneth, then the director of the Institut für Sozialforschung, for inviting me, to my surprise, to deliver these lectures and for thus giving me the opportunity to bring together the hitherto scattered pieces of the jigsaw puzzle of life. I would also like to thank all the scholars, whether permanent members of the Institut or occasional visitors, whose comments, questions, and criticisms have helped me to refine my thinking, particularly José Brunner, Thomas Khurana, Thomas Lemke, Yves Sintomer, Sarah Speck, Felix Trautmann, and Peter Wagner, who were joined later, in Paris, by Sandra Laugier, Guillaume Le Blanc, and Marielle Macé. I am also grateful to John Thompson for heartily supporting this book project, to Rachel Gomme for her elegant translation of the preamble and conclusion, and to Célia Chalfoun for her thorough revision of my initial version of the three chapters. Finally, since this book is nourished by several decades of academic research and human experience, I owe an incalculable debt to the many persons, particularly students and colleagues at the École des Hautes Études en Sciences Sociales in Paris and the Institute for Advanced Study in Princeton, but above all to those I have met in the course of my research, notably in South Africa and in France, who shared fragments of their life with me.

Princeton, February 2017

Note on the Illustration
of the Cover

Angelus Novus was painted by Paul Klee in 1920 using an oil transfer technique he had invented. It was purchased the following year by Walter Benjamin, who had it hung in the successive places where he lived and found in it an inspiration for several of his works, writing that having seen it could make the viewer "understand a humanity that proves itself by destruction." In the ninth thesis of his posthumous essay "on the philosophy of history," he describes it as the angel who, caught in a storm blowing from Paradise, contemplates the catastrophe of past events while being irresistibly propelled into the future. When he fled Germany in 1933, he brought it with him, but had to leave it in Paris with Georges Bataille, as he continued southwards to reach Spain. Just as he had crossed the border, in 1940, he was arrested and kept in custody in a hotel, where he was found dead the next day. At the end of the war, the artwork was passed with other possessions on to Theodor Adorno, who was at the time writing his *Minima Moralia*, before ending with Gershom Scholem, whose widow eventually gave it in 1987 to the Israel Museum, in Jerusalem. This "angel of history," as Benjamin called it, has therefore an intimate and lengthy relationship with the Frankfurt School, in its most tragic period. Coincidentally, the epigraph of the preamble of Georges Perec's *Life: A User's Manual* is a quotation by Paul Klee, which reads: "The eye follows the paths that have been laid down for it in the work." Let us, then, follow these paths.

Preamble

Minima Theoria

> If life fulfilled its vocation directly, it would miss it …
> Thought waits to be woken one day by the memory of
> what has been missed, and to be transformed into
> teaching.
>
> Theodor Adorno, *Minima Moralia*, 1974 [1951]

In the opening paragraph of his dedication to his friend and
colleague Max Horkheimer, of *Minima Moralia*, the bulk
of which was written in exile in the United States during
World War II, Theodor Adorno refers, with bitterness and
nostalgia, to "what the philosophers once knew as life."[1]
In modern societies, he continues, material production has
effectively reduced this life "to the rank of appendage," the
sphere of consumption offering no more than an "appearance of life," or rather, a "caricature of true life." In these
conditions, what he calls the "melancholy science" of the
thinkers of his time – an ironic reference to Nietzsche's
"gay science" – "relates to a region that from time imme-
morial was regarded as the true field of philosophy," but is
now "lapsed into intellectual neglect, sententious whimsy
and finally oblivion: the teaching of the good life." It is
worth pausing on the fact that the German expression *das
richtige Leben* is translated in French as *juste vie*: in fact,

the term has the dual sense of "good life" and "right life," illustrating a semantic tension present at the heart of moral philosophy, between the ethical relationship to the self and the ethical relationship to others.

However we interpret the term, this pessimistic observation by Adorno, the most significant figure in the first generation of the Frankfurt School and hence one of the founders of "critical social theory," sounds the death knell of the full moral life – whether it is said to be true, right, or good. All that remains is an "alienated form," whose impasses Adorno strives to demonstrate through a series of short, somber meditations on the most mundane facts and the most ordinary objects of the contemporary world. These meditations thus offer what Rahel Jaeggi calls "a critique of capitalism as a form of life," in other words, not only as unequal relations of production, but also as a degraded mode of existence: according to her, they put forward both "an ethics and a critique of ethics" – the possibility of a different life and the impossibility of bringing it into existence.[2] Indeed, Adorno's deliberately fragmentary reflections on the cultural practices of his era pose the question of what social and political preconditions would make it possible to institute "an order more worthy of human beings." Meanwhile, he acknowledges, we are far from that place, given that "our perspective of life has passed into an ideology which conceals the fact that there is life no longer." This is the manifestation of a "hopelessness" that is rendered all the more acute for being written in the shadows of the ruins of Nazi Germany.

Since Adorno's text was published, more than six decades have passed, and capitalism, which is now barely even mentioned by name – having been superseded by the ambiguous euphemism "neoliberalism" – seems still more triumphant and less contested than it was when Adorno wrote his essay. At the same time the tragic lessons of World War II and its genocides, which cast a painful shadow over the thinking of Adorno's contemporaries, seem to be fading as a politics of identity comes to the fore and authoritarian tendencies are exposed – the violence and uncertainty of a troubled world serving to legitimize all kinds of exclusion and repression. Worrying signs of a new "age of anxiety" – to borrow the title of W. H. Auden's long poem written during the same postwar period – these vicissitudes of democratic life affect human lives in profoundly differentiated and often unequal ways.[3] In other words, *Minima Moralia* has lost none of its pertinence, even if its analyses need to be adjusted to contemporary reality in order to ponder anew the "damaged life" of the book's subtitle. Here the paradox of Adorno's reflection needs to be emphasized. Faced with the enormity of the catastrophe of World War II and the Nazi regime's project of extermination, he makes what Miguel Abensour calls "the choice of the small," which "is inherently bound up with a revolt against the world of war and terror."[4] Hence the minimalist title; hence the shift of focus to the singularity of the individual; hence the affirmation of the relevance of philosophy as defense of life – whether true, right, or good.

In this book, I propose a different orientation, resituating individuals both in society and in the world: in society, that is, in the relational space that constitutes them; in the world, that is, in the global space within which they move. Rather than the disruptions of the ethical subject to which Adorno devotes his reflections, I attempt to grasp the tribulations of the political community. In place of the cultural developments he calls into question, I focus on deciphering structural facts. To this end, in place of Adorno's critique of ways of life, I propose a critique of the treatment of life and of lives, and more specifically of those vulnerable and precarious lives to which many human beings are reduced. My question is not: how are we living? Or, how should we live? But rather: what value do we attach to human life as an abstract concept? And how do we evaluate human lives as concrete realities? Any discrepancy or any contradiction between the evaluation of life in general and the devaluing of certain lives in particular then becomes indicative of a moral economy of life in contemporary societies.

By moral economy, I mean the production, circulation, appropriation, and contestation of values as well as affects, around an object, a problem, or more broadly a social fact – in this case, life. This concept borrows both from E. P. Thompson's analysis, in which he explains the eighteenth-century English food riots in terms of the moral economy of agricultural laborers (that is, in terms of the norms and social obligations that govern their expectations and their practices), and from Lorraine Daston's reading in her study of the production of knowledge in the seventeenth century, where she emphasizes the role of the moral economy of science (in other words, the values and affects shared by scientists).[5] I depart from these analyses, however, on several key points. Unlike Thompson, I do not restrict the moral economy purely to the domain of goods and services, but extend it to any social configuration that can be drawn on in the description of the moral state of the world: the way life is regarded and the way lives are treated provide the most powerful tools to analyze it. In contrast to Daston, I am interested less in a stable order around which a consensus is established than in the variations in values and affects over time, and how they enter into tension or competition with one another: evolutions and contradictions in the way life is valued in the abstract, and the way concrete lives are evaluated, are at the core of my thesis. Moreover, where Thompson expresses his own moral preferences, my analysis of moral principles and sentiments attempts to reveal and interpret them rather than judge them; and where Daston takes a cultural approach, I strive to grasp the social thinking and the relations of power underlying the production, circulation, appropriation, including the misappropriation, and contestation, even rejection, of values and affects. Moral economy as I conceive of it is not the moral economy of a group or a domain, but the moral economy of what makes sense in a given society at a given moment. In this respect, life, of which Adorno laments the eclipse, has perhaps never before been the focus of so many heterogeneous and contradictory moral investments. It is to the moral economy of life, understood in this sense, that this essay is devoted.

But do we really know what we are talking about, when we talk about life? This is far from certain, and we therefore need to consider the meaning of the word itself.

"Life is a term, none more familiar. And one almost would take it for an affront, to be asked what he meant by it," writes John Locke. But he immediately adds: "And yet, if it comes in question, whether a plant, that lies ready formed in the seed, have life; whether the embryo of an egg before incubation, or a man in a swoon without sense or motion, be alive, or no? it is easy to perceive, that a clear distinct settled idea does not always accompany the use of so known a word, as that of life is."[6] For Locke, then, the problem is above all that of determining the limits of life: its indistinct beginning in the seed or the egg (around which arguments continue today, in debates about voluntary termination of pregnancy), and its uncertain end in unconsciousness without feeling or movement (questions that would be subsequently raised around the recognition of brain death).

But the attempt to define "life" also raises concerns of a different order, bound up with the multitude of meanings encompassed by the word itself. It denotes at once a property of organized beings, a set of biological phenomena, a time that elapses between birth and death, and a range of events that fill this temporal space, to say nothing of metonymic or metaphorical uses when we refer, for instance, to the lives of great men, or the life of objects. Are we talking about the same thing in each case? Is the life of a human being a fact of the same order as the life of the cells that form the body? To be sure, the common-sense understanding does not tangle itself up in complications, and everyone understands more or less what is meant, amid the multifarious senses of the term, by expressions such as "life sciences," "life expectancy," "life in the country," or the "life of ideas," in each of which the word has a different meaning. The same cannot be said, however, of philosophers, who appear at an impasse when attempting to consider, for example, life as conceived by a biologist together with life as interpreted by a novelist.

The problem is articulated with clarity by Georges Canguilhem: "Perhaps it is not possible, even today, to go beyond this first notion: any experiential datum that can be described in terms of a history contained between its birth and its death is alive, and is the object of biological knowledge."[7] This seems a simple definition. Yet it brings together quite heterogeneous elements, which highlight a semantic tension. Knowledge and experience, biology and history: this is the great dualism inherent to life. And Hannah Arendt points to a similar duality: "Limited by a beginning and an end, that is, by the two supreme events of appearance and disappearance within the world, it follows a strictly linear movement whose very motion nevertheless is driven by the motor of biological life which man shares with other living things and which forever retains the cyclical movement of nature. The chief characteristic of this specifically human life, whose appearance and disappearance constitute worldly events, is that it is itself always full of events which ultimately can be told as a story, establish a biography."[8] Cyclical movement of nature and worldly events, biology and biography: these are the two series that make life an entity at once overdetermined in its material dimension and indeterminate in its course. In effect, one incorporates humans into a vast community of living beings, on the same level as animals and plants, while the other makes them exceptional living beings by virtue of their capacity for consciousness and language.

Can this binarism be resolved? Is it possible to think of life as biology and life as biography simultaneously? For 2,000 years, philosophers have applied themselves to this question. They have successively considered life as animation of matter, following Aristotle, as a mechanism generating movement, with Descartes, and as a self-maintaining organism, according to Kant. They thus moved from a vitalist representation to a mechanistic interpretation, and finally to an organicist approach, each with a different medium: the soul or breath, then the body and fluids, and finally the organs and the internal milieu.

However, the point in each of these various readings was to pursue an interrogation of the relationship between the living and the human, between the infrastructure of the former and the superstructure of the latter, as it were. For Hegel in particular, " 'life' is a transitional concept that relates the realm of nature to the realm of freedom," as Thomas Khurana puts it,[9] since while it is constrained by biological elements it can, through a process of self-organization, produce the autonomy required for the realization of a biographical journey.

In contrast to these earlier attempts to articulate the two dimensions of life, the opposition between the two trends has hardened during the last century, and particularly during recent decades, leading to an apparently irremediable division between the two.

As regards life in the biological sense, it is in the mid-twentieth century that the study of living beings shifted in scale, and hence also in perspective, through the unlikely intervention of quantum mechanics theorist Erwin Schrödinger.[10] Henceforth, the physicist turns biologist, his analysis descending to the molecular level, his method borrowing from thermodynamics, and atomic structure becoming a code whose innumerable permutations make possible the diversity of living beings and the creation of order out of entropic chaos. While validating this theory, the discovery of the DNA double helix a few years later constituted the foundation for a new conception of life, now based on information and its replication. And half a century later, the decoding of the human genome has further refined this concept. Even contemporary epigenetics does not fundamentally challenge this paradigm, since the

influence of context on genetic inheritance, which it seeks
to account for, operates through molecular mechanisms
that modify the expression of genes. In other words, biochemistry and biophysics, which are now integral strands
of biology, produce theories based on an increasingly
intensive molecularization of the living matter, albeit not
excluding systemic approaches at a higher level of complexity in microbial populations.[11] At the same time,
research into the origins of life focuses both on the emergence of living beings on Earth during the Precambrian
period and on the possibility of finding signs of life elsewhere in the universe. This research strives to understand
how inert molecules were able to transform into organic
molecules with the capacity to replicate themselves so as
to generate nucleic acids, and seeks to assemble spectral
libraries drawn from living terrestrial organisms. On the
one hand, microbiologists are searching for the "last universal common ancestor" of all cells, and the environment
conducive to its transformation. On the other hand, astrobiologists seek "potential biosignature gases" that would
point to the presence of life on the exoplanets of other
solar systems.[12] In both cases, science comes to meet the
imagination of men and women, and the prospect of dis-
covering the ultimate origin of life, or signs of extrater-
restrial life, even in the form of molecules rather than
identifiable beings, inspires dreams – and drives requests
for funding. In short, in the exploration of life as biological
phenomenon, the shift from conjecture to experiment,
from the macroscopic to the microscopic, and from bodies
to molecules, has progressively reduced the understanding
of life to its most basic material unit – an assemblage of
atoms – while simultaneously expanding it massively in
time and space: human beings are, indeed, dissolved in a
temporo-spatial network of molecular components of life
which appeared several billion years ago and may be
present in other parts of the universe.

   With life as biography, we find a quite different story
– more fragmentary, less cumulative. We can, however,

identify certain moments, such as the arrival of the novel in literature, and some features, including an increasingly anxious questioning as to how one should write about life and lives. On the one hand, the novel, as it developed from the eighteenth century onwards, constituted life for the first time not only as an interesting subject but also as a "detachable thing," as Heather Keenleyside puts it in her discussion of *Tristram Shandy*.[13] It frames life as a more or less linear unfolding of events, through which the subjectivities of the characters are formed, whether in Jane Austen's novels of manners, Goethe's Bildungsroman, or a little later, the great literary projects of Balzac and Zola, who reconstitute a society at a particular time through the life stories of individual characters more or less connected to each other. In its most complete as well as most radical expression, the autobiographical account becomes, with Proust, life itself, a life magnified by the creative labor of writing: this is what he calls true life, the life that, by virtue of convention and habit, we risk passing over, to the extent that one might die without ever having recognized it.[14] On the other hand, in the social sciences, from the very beginning, alongside the important developments in theory and methodology by the founders of the discipline, the life story has played a central part, whether it be reconstituting the trajectory of a Polish peasant, in the case of William Thomas and Florian Znaniecki, or recounting the history of a Mexican family, as does Oscar Lewis.[15] But it is particularly from the 1980s onwards that, as the reaction against structuralism came together with feminist critique and postcolonial studies, the demand arose, in anthropology as elsewhere, for recognition of individuals, their history, their truth, and their words.[16] The narrative turn was also a subjectivist turn. One should no longer speak in the name of subalterns, but rather make their voice heard – with the singular difficulty, particularly for historians, that their lives have often disappeared without leaving a trace in the archives.[17] But a few decades later, a contestation of the life story and its identification with real life began to emerge, both in literature, through a deconstruction of the narrative form in Samuel Beckett's work, and in the social sciences, in the form of Pierre Bourdieu's challenge to the biographical illusion.[18] Life as a coherent form became an object of suspicion.

Two life lines, then. For the purposes of clarity rather than classification, let us call the first one naturalist, the second humanist. My aim, in attempting this brief description of how they developed, is to point out the existence of two approaches that appear, at least in the first analysis, increasingly irreconcilable. The life studied by the biophysicist no longer bears any relation to that imagined by the novelist, even if some novelists incorporate biological elements into the fabric of their narratives, and some biologists venture, with varying success, into literature. The objects astrobiologists deal with, namely the molecules that indicate a presence of life, bear little relation to the subjects encountered by sociologists, namely individuals who recount the facts of their lives, even if, in the first case, the search for some presence of life is not unconcerned with the search for non-human intelligence, and, in the second, sociologists can make the life-sciences laboratory the focus of their research. We are far from the Aristotelian, Cartesian, Kantian, and Hegelian projects. In fact, the philosophical gesture of Hannah Arendt and Giorgio Agamben, who institute a fundamental distinction between *zoë* and *bios*, between the simple fact of being alive and the rich fulfillment of a life, could be interpreted as a way of politically marking the impossibility, and indeed the danger, of binding the two life lines in a single word and a single mode of thinking.[19] Both Arendt and Agamben saw, in the contemporary world, a fatal risk that the simple fact of being alive would increasingly supplant the rich fulfillment of a life.

It has to be acknowledged that what was perhaps the last attempt to devise a philosophy of life that could integrate the two dimensions, to wit the German *Lebensphilosophie* of the early twentieth century, was not unproblematic, either epistemologically or ethically.[20] Born out of Dilthey's hermeneutics of life, inspired equally by Nietzschean vitalism and by Bachofen's evolutionism, this theory put forward by Ludwig Klages and Alfred Baeumler derived from a strange combination of esthetic glorification of the irrational forces of life and a pedagogical urge to teach the good life. While it exerted a certain fascination over German intellectuals, including Walter Benjamin, it also influenced and nurtured the racial politics of national socialism, particularly since some of those who propounded it were appointed to important positions by the regime. It is, moreover, clearly with this "philosophy of life" that Adorno is vehemently taking issue at the beginning of *Minima Moralia*: he calls it an ideology that passes over the true life. It is, then, not in this anti-intellectual and anti-modern version that the reconciliation of life as fact of nature and life as fact of experience is to be sought.

Considering these vicissitudes of the concept, is an anthropology of life imaginable, or even desirable? Here we have to start from a paradox. Although anthropologists have always been interested in the lives of their interlocutors, in terms of both way of life and life stories, they have rarely made those lives a specific and legitimate object of their research. The lives that they studied synchronously, through the culture within which they unfolded, or diachronically, through the stories that reconstructed them, served as empirical material for their analysis of kinship, myths, social structures, religious practices, or political institutions. Even in its most embodied manifestations, such as biographies, the aim was principally to understand trajectories, situations, emotions. Life itself was rarely seen as an object of knowledge on the same level as the other categories constituting their discipline. It was a sort of vehicle or medium that allowed them access to concepts and realities deemed more significant or more relevant for the description and interpretation of societies.

In recent decades, however, anthropologists have started to construe life as object, principally considered in either the naturalist or the humanist form described above. On the one hand, within the context of the vast body of research emerging from the social studies of science, life has been approached as it is explored by researchers in the biological, physical, and even information sciences – as living matter. Anthropologists have analyzed the knowledge, practices, and matters of life sciences, focusing among other things on genomics and epigenetics, stem cells and cell death, hereditary conditions and regenerative medicine, the development of artificial intelligence and the use of neuroscience in criminology.[21] In other words, they have been endeavoring to understand and interpret the leading-edge research in terms of the various manifestations of life. On the other hand, in the more traditional domain of social or cultural anthropology, there has been a proliferation of monographs on the life of individuals based on the ordinary detail of their existence, in geographical contexts that vary widely but are often marked by the ordeals of poverty, sickness, and misfortune. There have been studies focused on the death of children in Brazilian favelas and the affliction of extreme poverty in rural India, on the destitution of the Ayoreo Indians of Paraguay and suicide among the Inuit of northern Canada, on the feeling of loss in the aftermath of the civil war in Sierra Leone and the tribulations of wounded veterans returning from war in the United States.[22] In these studies, life is generally presented not only in its subjective dimension, as experienced by these men and women, but also in terms of the objective conditions through which society contributes to shaping and treating it. In other words, apart from a few attempts to combine the naturalist and humanist approaches, for example in medical anthropology, where sickness sits at the meeting point of biology and biography,[23] the two life lines have largely been deployed as parallel avenues of anthropological research.

Yet these approaches are not conceived as anthropologies of life as such, but rather as anthropologies of life sciences and of life experiences respectively. However, several recent offerings diverge from this pattern. The first project is phenomenological. Countering an anthropology that considers life as having a beginning and an end, Tim Ingold asserts that it is possible to "restore anthropology to life" by considering that life "is a movement of opening, not of closure" – in other words, that it does not stop, but keeps on going.[24] Human beings are the producers of their own lives. Hence they also create history, which is itself caught up in the process of evolution; life, then, needs to be thought of as a line or a set of lines incorporated in these varying time scales, along which living beings take a sort of journey. The anthropologist's task is to account for this primacy of movement, for the way in which humans perceive the world, connect to their environment, manufacture objects and create stories, walk, breathe, and think. The second project is ontological. Distancing himself from what is suggested by the etymology of the word designating his discipline, Eduardo Kohn proposes an "anthropology beyond the human," that is, a radical decentering of the humanist perspective, on the basis of which it is possible to assert that in Amazonia, where he conducts his research, "dogs dream" and "forests think."[25] For him, it is no more appropriate to conceive the world through the representations that humans make of it than to think that humans occupy a special place in that world. This "anthropology of life" presupposes that all living beings, whether they belong to the physical environment or to the realm of the spirits, should be given the same consideration, in other words that we need to recognize that they enter into relation with one another through signs, and that they are endowed with a capacity to signify independently of humans. This is not an ethical standpoint, as formulated by moral philosophy and political ecology when they plead for animal rights or protection of the planet, but an epistemological statement, which asserts a different way of understanding the world. The third project is culturalist. Proposing to "take life as object," Perig Pitrou

invites anthropologists to "study how different peoples
conceive of the functional characteristics of living beings,
but also how they assign causes to these phenomena,"
since "each culture has its own way of categorizing the
elements and processes associated with the phenomena of
life, whether they are manifested in the human person or
in the environment."[26] Concretely, the proposed endeavor
is to "examine systematically local conceptions of growth,
reproduction, aging, scarring, adaptation," without reduc-
ing life "either to a substance that circulates between
bodies or to observable characteristics or behaviors," but
rather focusing on "the underlying theories that allow
people to understand the origins of these phenomena."
Further development of this approach, which recalls that
of the ethnosciences, could lead on to a "comparatist
approach" challenging the way life is interpreted in the
West. It is obviously tempting to add to these three frameworks the biopolitical paradigm developed by Michel Foucault but, as we shall see, far from being a politics of life
as the word suggests, biopolitics is in fact the government
of populations.

Considering these three intellectual projects, it is clear
that beyond their shared ambition of establishing an
anthropology of life, they are based on theories that are
not just different, but incompatible. Besides, and perhaps
more problematically, despite the innovative viewpoints
they suggest, they all pass over, to varying degrees, that
which constitutes the singularity of human life, namely the
tension between biology and biography, and the belonging
to social and cultural worlds that are always specific. For
example, the phenomenological project oscillates between
inscribing life in the long chain of evolution, and the
abstract description of desocialized movements, forms,
and spaces. Similarly, the ontological project includes all
living beings in its resolutely post-humanist description of
the world, but eschews historical and political analysis in
favor of pure semiotics. Finally, the culturalist project clings
to local theories that allow people to account for various

aspects of life, but privileges representations over practices, and conceptual frameworks over moral concerns. A totalizing approach aimed at constituting an anthropology of life thus seems doomed to failure, or at least to abandoning what we might call the humanity of life – the social, historical, political, and moral dimensions of human lives as they emerge from both living matter and lived existence. It was no doubt a similar observation that led Veena Das and Clara Han to put together an eclectic body of work around the theme of living and dying, in order, they write, to "trace the multiple paths" available for "anthropological explorations in the investigation of life and how it is conjoined to death in specific, concrete ways."[27] Their edited volume thus brings together contributions relating to biomedicine and biopolitics, pregnancy and adoption, suffering and suicide, sickness and mortality, ethics and religion.

Rather than this rich mosaic, I prefer, however, the modesty of a jigsaw puzzle whose few pieces adjust to each other and complement one another to form a coherent picture. As Georges Perec writes of this "thin art," in the foreword to *Life: A User's Manual*, "in isolation, a puzzle piece means nothing," but "as soon as you have succeeded in fitting it into one of its neighbors," "the two pieces so miraculously conjoined are henceforth one."[28] This is the method Perec himself uses as he gradually reconstitutes the lives of the inhabitants of the apartment block located at 11 Rue Simon-Crubellier in Paris. The end result of his exercise "is not a sum of elements" but "a pattern, that is to say a form, a structure." Ultimately, "the parts do not determine the pattern, but the pattern determines the parts," and "the pieces are readable, take on a sense, only when assembled." Yet despite the fact that it now forms a single whole, the jigsaw puzzle retains the memory of its plural aspect, which can be discerned in the subtle lines separating the pieces that make it up. The key to this plurality is offered in the book's unusual subtitle, in the French version: *Romans* – Fictions.

In order to render an account of life that does justice to the complexity of its multiple dimensions while at the same time representing it with a degree of unity, I therefore propose to analyze and relate three conceptual elements: forms of life, ethics of life, and politics of life. Each of these opens up an anthropological fact of life. Thus, beyond the contradictory interpretations proposed by exegetes, forms of life, as outlined by Wittgenstein, reveal the tension between the specific modes of existence and a common condition of humanity. The experience of refugees and migrants offers a tragic illustration. Unlike the concept of the ethical life inherited from Greek philosophy, ethics of life extend Walter Benjamin's reflection on the sacralization of life as supreme good. The higher principle of humanitarian morality that consists in saving people threatened by disaster, epidemic, famine, or war here collides with the opposite rationale based on the honor of sacrificing oneself for a cause on the battlefield, in a suicide attack, or by hunger strike. Finally, taking up an illuminating idea that was never fully followed through, politics of life reformulates Foucault's notion of biopolitics. The inquiry reveals that the actual evaluation of lives contradicts the abstract valuation of life since one puts different monetary value on human existences depending on social categories, and since one considers that some deserve to live more than others.

So if it is true, as Perec suggests, that it is the pattern that determines the parts rather than the opposite, the theoretical framework behind each of these three concepts derives from a reflection on the treatment of human lives in contemporary societies. One theme underlies this reflection: inequality. As I will show, this theme binds together the biological and the biographical, the material and social dimensions of life – in other words, the naturalist and the humanist approaches. What I propose, then, is not an anthropology of life, which I deem an impossible project, but rather an anthropological composition formed of three elements which when assembled, like a jigsaw puzzle, reveal an image: the inequality of human lives.

Each of the three concepts proposed derives from a relatively specific philosophical heritage. And each of them has been more or less faithfully adopted in the social sciences, particularly in anthropology. It is naturally within this latter register that I shall situate my analysis, but I shall do so in continual dialogue with the philosophers whose works have accompanied me over the course of the years. Yet, this transdisciplinary conversation is a delicate exercise. It is open to misunderstandings that I want to articulate and, I hope, clarify straightaway.[29] Concepts from one type of knowledge cannot be applied literally in another. Such an approach, of which there are plentiful examples among the philosophical borrowings in the social sciences, generally leads to the alteration of empirical results and the sterilization of theoretical reflection – probably the ultimate unfaithfulness to the original.

In this respect, translating from one discipline into another is very similar to translating from one language into another. In the latter case, it is generally recognized that the art of translation presupposes a degree of poetic license, even of literary violence – what Philip Lewis calls an "abusive translation," though he notes ironically that the English term, with its connotations of the violence done to meaning, carries a sense very different from what is conveyed by the French form *traduction abusive*, which denotes rather a failure to abide by the rules.[30] If, then, we are to develop a fruitful exchange between philosophy and the social sciences, how are we to get beyond the choice between a literalism that reifies concepts and an alteration that betrays them? According to George Steiner, the "hermeneutic motion" of translation is fourfold: trust, which implies the acknowledgment that there is something worth understanding; aggression, which is manifested through an extraction aimed at grasping it; incorporation, which involves a more or less complete assimilation in a new context; and finally restitution, which consists in a restoration that compensates for the violation and loss.[31] As with literary works, with which Steiner is concerned in this hermeneutic motion, the understanding and appropriation of a philosophical theory proceed from complex logics that bring into play these various aspects of exchange – a singular modality of gift and counter-gift, or perhaps of transference and counter-transference, in which a certain degree of betrayal may be the highest expression of respect for the author.

It is in this spirit that I propose to reinterpret forms of life, to turn from the ethical life to ethics of life, and to replace biopolitics with politics of life. As I do so, however, I shall take time at each stage to examine these theories, before engaging them, on the basis of my empirical research, in order to develop alternative or complementary readings. This research can thus be regarded as a way of testing concepts. Having conducted a range of mainly ethnographic studies in sub-Saharan Africa, Latin America, and Europe over two decades, I shall nevertheless concentrate, for the purposes of coherence, on the parallels between South Africa and France around situations, scenes, and narratives that open up ways of grasping the issues concerning life. But I shall also draw on other approaches – genealogical, historiographic, sociological, and demographic – on the premise that it is from the encounter between their different methods that the social sciences derive their empirical validity and theoretical relevance.

I

Forms of Life

Life forms a surface that acts as if it could not be
otherwise, but under its skin things are pounding and
pulsing.

Robert Musil, *The Man Without Qualities*,
1995 [1930]

How can human life be distinguished from the life of other
animals, and even from lower manifestations of life? And
to what extent is this life affected by the multiple ways of
being human produced through the infinite variations of
the social milieu, the cultural background or the historical moment? In other words, how should we characterize human life to account for commonalities with other
expressions of the living as well as differences among
human groups in space and time, which seem to dissolve
its singularity and its unity, respectively? This dual questioning has been, at least since Aristotle, at the heart of
philosophical reflection, which is in large part anthropological, that is, a discourse on the human. It has, however,
benefited from a renewed interest during the past decades
with the rediscovery of Ludwig Wittgenstein's notion of
"form of life."

Barely outlined in his posthumous writings, this
notion has indeed given rise to multiple exegeses among

philosophers as well as, more recently, anthropologists. From the philosophy of language, where it was conceived, it has thus been imported into the social sciences and the humanities with diverse and more or less defined meanings to ponder on ways of being in the world. A crucial interpretive tension, which has led to diametrically opposed perspectives on forms of life, resides precisely in the response given to the initial two questions, and therefore in the relative importance attached to their invariable and natural aspect or, conversely, their variable and cultural side. Are forms of life shared by the whole human species or is it inscribed in a given space and time?

Rather than choosing between these two options, I propose to shift the issues in three complementary ways. I will first broaden the circle of authors engaged in the conversation by using the contributions of two philosophers who also took an interest in forms of life, Georges Canguilhem and Giorgio Agamben. I will then complicate the dualism between naturalist and humanist approaches by proposing three antagonistic couples, opposing the universal and the particular, the biological and the biographical, rule and practice. Finally, I will consider the discordances resulting from these confrontations between authors and between terms as productive tensions rather than insurmountable contradictions. To this end, I will empirically test this triple theoretical shift by using the research I have conducted in France and South Africa over the past 10 years on a particularly significant contemporary form of life, that of forced nomads, be they called refugees or migrants, asylum seekers or undocumented foreigners. Thus, I will offer a reframing of the idea of forms of life, more in phase with the ethics and politics of life.

The last text to which Michel Foucault gave his imprimatur before his death is an article titled "Life: Experience and Science."[1] A lightly revised version of the introduction to the English edition of *The Normal and the Pathological*, it was intended for publication as part of a special issue dedicated to his mentor at the École normale supérieure, Georges Canguilhem. Reflecting on the philosophical field after World War II, he identifies a "dividing line" that runs through all the other theoretical oppositions: "It is the one that separates a philosophy of experience, of meaning, of the subject, and a philosophy of knowledge, of rationality, of the concept." On one side, Sartre and Merleau-Ponty; on the other side, Cavaillès, Bachelard, Koyré, and Canguilhem. He adds: "Doubtless this cleavage comes from afar, and one could trace it back through the nineteenth century," with Bergson and Poincaré, Lachelier and Couturat, Maine de Biran and Comte. But there is a remarkable paradox in the fact that the practitioners of "the most theoretical, the most geared to speculative tasks, and the farthest removed from immediate political inquiries" philosophy have been the most directly involved in the Resistance "during the war" as well as in the social movements "in the sixties," as if "the question of the basis of rationality could not be dissociated from an interrogation concerning the current conditions of its existence." Making an unexpected connection, Foucault comments: "If one had to look outside France for something corresponding to the work of Koyré, Bachelard, Cavaillès and Canguilhem, it would be in the vicinity of the Frankfurt School, no doubt, that one would find it." Indeed, in both cases, the questions addressed have to do with "a rationality that aspires to the universal while developing within contingency" and with "a reason whose structural autonomy carries the history of dogmatisms and despotisms along with it." For the philosophers of these two seemingly so distant traditions, the conditions of the formation of knowledge would thus be at play. However, in the case of Canguilhem, the connection between these conditions and the corresponding knowledge is particularly crucial, as the living itself is the inherent condition to the formation of a body of knowledge on the living. "Phenomenology expected 'lived experience' to supply the originary meaning of every act of knowledge," Foucault writes. "But can we not or must we not look for it in the 'living' itself?" Should we not go even further and reverse the relation between the two terms, by making of this work of knowledge a real form of life? Indeed, "forming concepts is a way of living and not a way of killing life," because it is "to show, among those billions of living beings that inform their environment and inform themselves on the basis of it, an innovation that can be judged as one likes, tiny or substantial." In other words, life is inseparable from the knowledge of life, because the first is necessary to the second, and because the latter gives a meaning to the former. Being the last text proofread by Foucault, only two months before his death, this homage to the philosopher who was his thesis supervisor ends with the word "life."

But let us return to the source. How did Canguilhem envision this relation between life and knowledge of life, and what forms of life emerge from it? He dedicated two major works to this question 15 years apart.[2] In the first text, he justifies knowledge beyond itself: "Knowing only in order to know is hardly more sensible than eating in order to eat, killing in order to kill, or laughing in order to laugh, since it is at once an avowal – that knowledge must have a meaning – and a refusal to find in knowledge any meaning other than itself." Consequently, there must be a reason above knowledge production: "One enjoys not the laws of nature but nature itself." Therefore, it should be understood that "knowledge undoes the experience of life, seeking to analyze its failures so as to abstract from it both a rationale for prudence ... and, eventually, laws for success." For "life is the formation of forms" and "knowledge is the analysis of informed matter," which can thus "help man remake what life has made without him, in him, or outside of him." In short, for Canguilhem, to better understand the living is to improve life by making sense of its forms. In the second essay, he deepens his study of "the relations between concept and life" in light of new developments in biology, particularly genetics. This investigation brings him to distinguish "at least two questions," depending on whether one considers "the universal organization of matter" or "the experience of a particular being, man." This twofold dimension corresponds to two grammatical forms: "By 'life', one can understand the present participle and the past participle of the verb to live – the living and the lived." A clear hierarchy is established between the two: the second dimension is "commanded" by the first, which is "more fundamental." Indeed, without the material structure of the living there would undoubtedly be no experiential dimension of the lived. Nevertheless, even if Canguilhem devoted most of his work to the former, he endeavors not to dissociate it from the latter. One could even see, in the form of life he imagines, namely a life giving form to the biological – or, better, "a meaning inscribed in the matter" – an attempt to reconcile, albeit asymmetrically, the two lineages of philosophy according to Foucault: the combination of the living and the lived would be, so to speak, the alliance of science and experience. Nothing surprising to this, notes Canguilhem: after all, "do the theory of the concept and the theory of life not have the same age and the same author?" and "does this author not connect both to the same source?" Aristotle is indeed a logician and a naturalist. For him, "the concept of the living is the living" and "knowledge is rather the universe reflected within the soul than the soul reflecting on the universe." The two manifestations of life – the living matter and the lived experience – are therefore closely connected in a tension between the biological structure common to all human beings and the singular subjective existence of each of them.

It is with a much different perspective that, a few years earlier, Wittgenstein had approached this tension consubstantial to human condition when he discussed "forms of life." The expression appears, as is well known, only five times in his *Philosophical Investigations* and does not seem to have been designed as a concept.[3] According to Lynne Rudder Baker, this is neither a defect nor an oversight: the theoretical development of the expression would require

tools which are actually produced by the very forms of
life and which, therefore, cannot serve to analyze them.
"Since these scientific procedures presuppose the forms
of life that render them intelligible, they are not available
for the investigation of forms of life. One result is that
Wittgenstein does not use, cannot use, 'forms of life' as a
theoretical or explanatory concept."[4] Although the notion
is never defined or clarified, and although it may be interpreted in various ways, it is generally considered that forms
of life consist in an agreement in the ordinary language that
allows human beings to share common understandings in
most situations. However, even such a meaning leads to two
contradictory readings depending on whether one assigns
an invariant or a contextual nature to this agreement. As
Kathleen Emmett writes: "Wittgenstein's remarks about
'forms of life' can be interpreted in two startlingly different ways. The difference between them turns on whether
all human beings of every time and place have the same
forms of life or whether cultural and historical variations
among them are possible."[5] She calls the first interpretation, which she criticizes, "transcendental," and the second
one, which she supports, "anthropological," a terminology
proposed by Jonathan Lear, who takes the opposite view,
considering that forms of life exceed specific descriptions,
which render them inaccessible to social investigation as
they pertain to "nonempirical insight."[6] These opposing
interpretations actually lie on the understanding authors
have of the concept of agreement, which is central to Wittgenstein's notion of form of life: "Human beings ... agree
in the language they use. That is not an agreement in
opinions but in form of life." Ironically, exegetes of Wittgenstein's writings thus strongly disagree on the meaning
of a notion that precisely attempts to reflect the agreement
between human beings. However, this contradiction is not
really such, since, even for divergence to be expressed and
understood, there must be a common language.

   There are therefore two apparently incompatible families of thought around the idea of forms of life. For Bernard

Williams, there can only be one form of life, because for us to understand others, that is, to understand their practices, these "others" must already belong to the group we consider as "us."[7] Relativism is therefore an impossibility, as well as any investigation on forms of life: "Since the fact that our language is such and such, and that the world we live in is as it is, are transcendental facts, they have no empirical explanations." Being within a certain form of life, we cannot conceive of another, and were we to encounter one, we would not be able to apprehend it as such. For Stanley Cavell, conversely, there is a plurality of forms of life corresponding to contexts in which human beings understand each other within the terms of their ordinary language, be it verbal communication, body language or other.[8] It has to do with "our sharing routes of interest and feeling, modes of response, senses of humor and of significance and fulfillment, of what is outrageous, of what is similar to what else, what a rebuke, what a forgiveness, of when an utterance is an assertion, when an appeal, when an explanation." In fact, "human speech and activity, sanity and community, rest upon nothing more, but nothing less, than this." A form of life is therefore what allows us, in a given context, to share meanings and exist in a common world. It is not surprising that anthropologists – and more generally, social scientists – identify more with Cavell's version than with Williams's. Not only does it seem more open to both the recognition of cultural differences and the possibility of overcoming them, but it also acknowledges the necessity and importance of empirical work, which is essential to their scientific practice. In fact, they may even find support for their interpretive choice in the thought experiment that Wittgenstein proposes:[9] "If we use the ethnological approach does that mean we are saying philosophy is ethnology? No, it means we are taking up our position far outside, in order to see the things more objectively. One of my most important methods is to imagine a historical development of our ideas different from what has actually occurred." Thus, according to the

theorist of ordinary language, we can, at least in our imagination, approach other forms of life. This is what anthropologists devote themselves to, but they do so in the real
world, by interacting with other human beings.

Prima facie, the distance between Canguilhem and Wittgenstein could not be greater, to the point that what they
mean by "form of life" challenges the very idea of a heuristic confrontation. For Canguilhem, it has to do with the
organization of the matter. For Wittgenstein, it refers to
the condition of mutual understanding. "Life is the form
and the power of the living," affirms the former. "To
imagine a language means to imagine a form of life,"
asserts the latter.[10] Both use the term "grammar" to characterize their understanding of what a form of life is, but
for Canguilhem it is inscribed in the genetic code of human
species, ensuring their reproduction, while for Wittgenstein it is a convention allowing human beings to share
understandings. Both are interested in the meaning, but
one sees it in the structure of the living and the other in
language games. Two worlds definitely far removed from
each other. Interestingly, this theoretical division translates
into the anthropological field through a distinction that
the French *forme de vie* and the German *lebensform* do
not grasp but that the English expressions *life form* and
form of life acknowledge. Works on life forms have given
birth to a field of research named multispecies anthropology, which is interested in animals, from primates to bees,
and in plants, from forests to gardens, while studies of
forms of life have mostly focused on violence and suffering, which are regarded as ultimate tests for the humanity
of human beings.[11] What is at stake in this dualism between
naturalism and humanism, omnipresent in contemporary
anthropology, is the very place of the human: advocates of
the former plead for an intellectual revolution in the social
sciences, foretelling a post-human era, while champions of
the latter defend the ethical primacy of the human – a
debate with moral and political implications going way
beyond the social sciences.

Is this theoretical distance between Canguilhem's and Wittgenstein's forms of life – between structures of the living and language games – consequently as insuperable as it seems? In fact, if one analyzes their approaches – in other words, the movement of their thinking – rather than opposing the explicit meaning they give to the notion, a convergence is possible. Indeed, both attempt to reconcile the two opposite poles of forms of life: for Canguilhem, the matter and the experience; for Wittgenstein, the transcendent and the contextual. This endeavor appears explicitly in Canguilhem's work, but remains implicit, almost obscure, in Wittgenstein's, generating, as previously discussed, contradictory interpretations. The most significant attempt to reconcile the two poles can be found in Cavell's late writings.[12] For him, the dominant reading of Wittgenstein, which has correctly but restrictively focused on "the social nature of human language and conduct," and thus, the cultural aspect of forms of life, has led to a "partial eclipse of the natural," overlooking the implications of the notion on the commonality of mankind. To restore this neglected portion of forms of life, Cavell suggests distinguishing two dimensions. The first one, "ethnological" or "horizontal," emphasizes differences between societies, for example between "coronations and inaugurations, or between barter and a credit system." The second one, "biological" or "vertical," regards differences between human beings and other living beings, for example between "poking at your food, perhaps with a fork, and pawing at it, or pecking at it." These two dimensions are not simply complementary. They have a conflicting relation: "The biological interpretation of form of life is not merely another interpretation to that of the ethnological, but contests its sense of political or social conservatism." This distinction is therefore very different from the one that classically opposes the biological, viewed as what characterizes all living beings, and the biographical, viewed as what is specifically human. In Cavell's interpretation, the boundary is always between the human and the other species, as the ethnological dimension refers to what differentiates human beings, whereas the biological dimension serves to differentiate humans from other species. His approach thus requires that we draw from "the fact that I am a man" all the consequences pertaining to the "capacity for work, for pleasure, for endurance, for appeal, for command, for understanding, for wish, for will, for teaching, for suffering" rather than to the cultural singularities. The merit of this reinterpretation of forms of life is to shift the emphasis from the first to the second term of the phrase: from forms to life.

But should the two terms be separated, let alone opposed? Do we have to choose between forms and life? This is the central question posed by Giorgio Agamben in his study in historical philosophy about medieval monastic rules.[13] His thesis is that forms of life, in which "a life is linked so closely to its form that it proves to be inseparable from it," appeared in monasteries almost a thousand years ago. In fact, the concept of form of life was already present two decades earlier with a similar definition in a series of his essays on refugees and camps: "A life that can never be separated from its form, a life in which it is never possible to isolate something such as a naked life." Yet, 20 years later, when he returns to this trope, which he has actually never abandoned, he proposes three significant reorientations. First, he shifts from the genealogical to the historical, abandoning the emblematic figure of the early Roman Republic *homo sacer* to draw a comprehensive picture of the daily life of Franciscan friars in the Middle Ages. Second, he replaces the tragic paradigm of the refugee and the camp by the ordinary mode of existence of monks in their abbeys. Third, he substitutes the normative approach of a sovereignty on bare life with an analytical reading of rules constituting forms of life. These three major moves – from genealogy to history, from tragic to ordinary, and from normative to analytical – open new perspectives for a dialogue with the social sciences that has sometimes become difficult due to ambiguity, on one side, and incomprehension, on the other.

What does Agamben have to say on this version of forms of life? Long before philosophers started to discuss the concept at length, he argues, the expression was used by theologians. Although it appeared prior to the origins of monasticism, "it is only with the Franciscans that the syntagma *forma vitae* assumes the character of a genuine technical term of monastic literature and life as such becomes the question that is in every sense decisive." This evolution occurs in the thirteenth century with the introduction of the rule of Saint Francis. But Agamben's interest in this monastic form of life does not reside in "the imposing mass of punctilious precepts and ascetic techniques, of cloisters and horologia, of solitary temptations and choral liturgies, of fraternal exhortations and ferocious punishments through which cenoby constituted itself as a 'regular life' in order to achieve salvation." His focus lies instead on "the dialectic that comes to be established between the two terms rule and life." From this perspective, the Franciscans' most radical gesture is, through their vow of poverty, the abdication of every right, starting with that of property and even of use. As William of Ockham courageously argues before the ecclesial authorities of his time, in case of extreme necessity, friars have a "natural right" to use what is needed for their existence but no "positive right" to it. In other words, the Franciscans' revolutionary project consists in "the attempt to realize a human life and practice absolutely outside the determinations of the law." Hence the dispute and conflict with the secular clergy, the Curia, and eventually the Pope himself.

The Franciscans' form of life is not without contemporary equivalents. We can think, for instance, of the Jain renunciants in India, studied by James Laidlaw, or the Muslim women belonging to piety movements in Egypt, among whom Saba Mahmood conducted her research.[14] Beyond their apparent singularity, these religious forms of life, in which form and life are so closely linked that the

first gives meaning to the second, encourage us to reassess
the mediation played by the law – here the religious law
– between the individual and the collective, between body
and institution, between rule and life. That law is constitu-
tive of any form of life, even though it is so invisible that
its influence over our behavior does not appear clearly, has
been well established by legal consciousness theories,
according to which the experience of the social world
involves a relation with the law, which is itself closely connected to gender, social class, belonging to a minority,
etc.[15] What Agamben adds to these theories is the paradoxical extension of this relation to situations that are
outside the common legal space, even while obeying a rule.
More generally, we can say that forms of life are determined by the law, both within and without the legal framework. In the latter case, the relation to the law may even
be more decisive, whether it is rejected, as with Franciscans
in times past, anarchists not long ago, and civil disobedi-
ence activists nowadays, or it serves to exclude, as with
yesterday's banished and today's undocumented.

However, Agamben somewhat revises his view a few
years later as he moves away from the historical context
of the monastic experience and offers a more general formulation in which "a life that cannot be separated from
its form is a life for which, in its mode of life, its very living
is at stake, and, in its living, what is at stake is first of all
its mode of life."[16] In other words, what characterizes
"human life" is that the "modes, acts, and processes"
which constitute it "are never simply facts but always and
above all possibilities of life." In a sort of tacit dialogue
with Canguilhem and Wittgenstein, he states that "the
form of human living is never prescribed by a specific
biological vocation nor assigned by any necessity whatso-
ever" and defines as "thought the connection that constitutes forms of life into an inseparable context ... in which
it is never possible to isolate something like a bare life."
In these fragmentary reflections, Agamben tries above all
to insist on "the potential character of life." Inasmuch as

it is human, a form of life is always an exploration of possibilities.

Having examined at some length what appears to be, at first sight, a heterogeneous philosophical corpus, we are left with a question: how can such a discussion enrich our understanding of forms of life? By imagining this conversation between deeply dissimilar theories with singular genesis and parallel developments, I tried to operate a double rupture with regard to dominant approaches to forms of life in the humanities and the social sciences. First, rather than a choice between transcendental and anthropological readings, which has divided the field of Wittgensteinian studies, I propose a dialectical approach which allows their confrontation: to the alternative between incompatible paradigms, I prefer the productive tension between what abolishes differences and what recognizes them. Second, instead of giving exclusive prominence to Wittgensteinian writings, as most authors do, I believe it is heuristic to put them in relation to others: new perspectives thus become open to analysis.

Based on these principles, I will explore a triple tension, drawn from the distinctions present to various degrees in Wittgenstein's, Canguilhem's, and Agamben's writings: between universal and particular (the transcendental vs. the anthropological); between biology and biography (the living vs. the lived); between law and practice (rule vs. freedom). Nevertheless, I want to add to this triple dialectic a dual dimension – political and moral – that is scarcely present in these three versions of the forms of life. It is well known that Wittgenstein kept his distance from both, while Canguilhem was probably more sensitive to them in his personal engagements than in his scientific work. Finally, even though Agamben puts the foundation of politics at the heart of his intellectual project, which also includes, more or less explicitly, a moral concern, his theory of forms of life only incorporates them marginally at a later stage. However, this relative absence has recently been corrected in some works focusing particularly on social

movements and the practices of care.[17] But the approach
that I will develop, based on the empirical research I have
conducted in France and South Africa, follows another
path: I will describe and analyze a form of life haunting
the collective imagination of contemporary societies, that
of transnational precarious nomads – refugees or migrants,
asylum seekers or undocumented foreigners.

Calais, in the North of France, became notorious world-
wide for its so-called "jungle," a vast camp built on a
wasteland at the margins of the town, where thousands of
refugees and migrants were gathered in 2014. Indeed, since
the 1980s, the area had been the gateway for successive
waves of people fleeing various conflict-affected regions
east and south of Europe and aiming to reach Britain:
initially Vietnamese; later Tamils, Kosovars, Kurds, and
Afghans; more recently Sudanese, Eritreans, Libyans, and
Syrians. In 1999, after the United Kingdom began to
enforce a stricter control of its border, thus preventing
people from crossing the Channel, the number of refugees
and migrants around Calais rapidly increased, and a warehouse was opened by the French socialist government with
the assistance of the Red Cross. Initially a transit center,
Sangatte rapidly transformed into a temporary housing
settlement as people were prevented from continuing their
odyssey. In 2002, when the conservative party in France
returned to power, one of the first decisions that the new
minister of the interior took was to close the center, officially due to security issues and humanitarian concerns.
From then on, refugees and migrants were left with no
other option than to squat in public spaces, abandoned
buildings, and even bunkers overlooking the beach, odd
vestiges of World War II. Their living conditions were all
the more precarious given the fact that the police harassed
them continually, dislodging them from their makeshift
shelters in the middle of the night regardless of weather
conditions, and destroying their meager belongings. This
situation persisted for a dozen years.

With the civil war raging in Libya and Syria, the number of refugees and migrants from Africa and the Middle East suddenly increased around Calais in 2014. Confronted with this new crisis, the left-leaning government took the decision to relocate them on a former dump site close to two chemical plants that rendered the place barely usable: squalid and insalubrious, it had no electricity and no water. Yet non-governmental organizations, mostly from France and England, worked on making the site habitable and soon put up tents, assembled shacks, installed toilets, brought food, created a health clinic, a legal center, a library, a school, and even a theater, while residents opened stores, restaurants, and barber shops, and erected a church and a mosque. Every night, hundreds of men and women tried at the peril of their lives to reach England through the Channel Tunnel or the Port of Calais. The tally of identified casualties in the surroundings of the latter amounted to 19 in 2014 and 25 in 2015.[18] The gradual addition of cameras, high walls, electric fences, the multi-plication of vehicle checks, and the implementation of carbon dioxide detectors had indeed reduced the chances of success but increased the risks of accidents. During the crossing attempts, the police brutally intervened with their dogs and tear gas. According to a survey, eight residents out of ten stated having been subjected to violence by law enforcement agents and half of them claimed to have been arrested and detained.[19] Disheartened but determined to try again, they returned at dawn to the camp, which was sometimes still surrounded by the remains of smoke from nightly clashes with the police. Three-quarters of the residents considered the place unsafe, first and foremost due to the threatening presence of heavily armed and frequently aggressive officers around the camp. In March 2016, in a desperate gesture of protest against the inflexibility of the French government which, disregarding a court decision, had undertaken the destruction of their shelters, eight Iranian refugees decided to sew their lips together and to put on a blindfold while carrying placards reading "We

are human beings," "Where is our freedom?" and "I came
here to find my human rights but I have found none."
These men did not understand why they could not benefit
from the protection of states that had, for decades, systematically denounced the human rights violations committed
by the Iranian regime.

Having conducted research in Sangatte in the early
2000s, I returned to Calais in January 2016, a few weeks
before the French government decided to raze the camp to
the ground, notwithstanding the fact that the wretched
dwellings had been built on the very land provided by the
authorities a year before.[20] At the time, the jungle hosted
an estimated 5,500 persons, almost exclusively young
men. I had the opportunity to speak with some of them,
one of these conversations being with a small group of
Syrians, in the shack they used as temporary housing. The
walls were covered on the outside with a blue plastic
canvas that hardly prevented the rain from seeping in, and
on the inside with aluminum foil that let the cold air pen-
etrate all the same. The six-square-meter place sheltered
six young men, four of whom were undergraduate students, as was the case for more than a third of the residents
in the camp. They were from a region controlled by rebel
groups and regularly bombed by the loyalist air force. As
the troops of the Baathist regime advanced toward their
town, they had left Syria to avoid being confronted with
the alternative of repression by or conscription in Bashar
al-Assad's army. After having traveled across Europe to
reach Great Britain, their journey had come to a stop in
Calais. They had lived in the jungle for between one and
three months. They did not speak French and in light of
what they had learnt about France since their arrival, they
were not tempted to stay. Their hope was, as for many
others, to reach England where all had relatives or friends
who had settled there.

Considering the mud present everywhere in the camp,
both the shack and the clothes hanging on nails hammered
into the walls were surprisingly clean, and in view of the

human density of the place, its orderly character was remarkable. Notwithstanding their extreme destitution, the young men apologized for not being able to offer me tea, and one of them even went out to get free soup from a local charity, but came back empty-handed. Wrapped in their sleeping bags, they were speaking softly but with excitement; they seemed eager to communicate their anxieties and expectations. They explained that they were going out at night and sleeping during the day. Almost every evening since they had arrived in the camp, they had been trying to cross the Channel without success. Each time, they had been chased by the police and their dogs, often beaten, occasionally arrested. As evidence, two of them exhibited recent wounds and scars on their legs and arms. But what they wanted to bear witness to above all concerned their previous life in Syria. One after the other, they showed me the photos that they preciously kept in their smartphones. The sequence was always the same: first, images of their relatives, girlfriend, house, car, which bore witness to their life before the war; then, images of massacres and destructions, the dead bodies of a father, brother, young cousin, and the rubble of what had been their neighborhood. Yet they were not appealing to compassion: they seemed to be sharing these memories of a recent past in order to stress the indignity of their present situation. The pictures representing them elegantly dressed in front of the affluent family house attested to a previous economic status that contrasted with the conditions in which they were now living. Those revealing the tragedies they had gone through rendered the brutal treatment by the French authorities disquieting and indefensible. Never would they have thought, they repeated, that they would end up one day in the middle of the winter sleeping on the ground in a wasteland, and being constantly harassed by the police of a country which they believed to be welcoming.

After we parted, as I was strolling across tents and shacks, I noticed a stencil by the English street artist Banksy on the concrete pile of the bridge that towered over the camp and marked its entrance. It represented Steve Jobs, whose biological father was Syrian, carrying a bundle of clothes on his shoulder and a computer in his hand. At his feet, someone had gathered dozens of remnants of tear-gas grenades which formed a sort of altar ironically honoring the French state's repression...

Some 9,000 kilometers from there, in the Central Business District of Johannesburg, dozens of sumptuous edifices, once symbols of the South African opulence, where multinational companies had their head offices and the white upper class their residence, have been abandoned by their occupants in the years following the end of apartheid in 1994 and are now squatted by illegal dwellers. They are known as "dark buildings" and house thousands of asylum seekers and undocumented foreigners, mostly from neighboring countries, living in dire conditions and paying rents to local gangs. Among these migrants, the majority, from the early 2000s onwards, were Zimbabweans fleeing the repression of Robert Mugabe's authoritarian regime, the economic crisis that followed the confiscation of white farmlands, and the international sanctions implemented in response. It is estimated that close to 2 million people crossed the border between the two countries in a little over 10 years. This massive displacement added to the flow of people coming from Central and Southern Africa, most of them also fleeing war and poverty. According to the United Nations High Commissioner for Refugees, there were, all nationalities combined, 15,000 asylum seekers in 2000; 170,000 in 2010; 800,000 in 2015.[21] The country then ranked first globally with a third of the asylum seekers in the world.

These figures cannot be explained by the number of petitioners alone. They are also the consequence of extremely long processing times. Indeed, although after the advent of democracy the South African government had committed itself to respecting the international law flouted by the former regime, particularly regarding asylum, the demographic pressure and the inefficacy of the bureaucratic process in place quickly led to a backlog. When they were completed, procedures had often lasted more than five years, including the lodging of the appeal when the case was rejected – by far the most frequent outcome.[22] During this interminable period of uncertainty, claimants had to renew their application every six months in a reception center. This requirement involved unpleasant lengthy waiting lines that forced people to spend several days and nights in the center or to bribe the agents to arrange an earlier appointment. With years passing, many of them, discouraged, eventually gave up and since their permits were no longer valid, became undocumented aliens. The official recognition of the right to asylum combined with the multiplication of obstacles in its implementation had two contradictory effects: on the one hand, the slow process led to a congestion of the system, which automatically increased the number of petitioners; but on the other hand, the dissuasive practices used by the administration led many claimants to give up their application procedure, which resulted in an artificial decrease in the statistics. Not surprisingly, in 2016, the official data were contested by non-governmental organizations which were concerned about the hostile reactions against asylum seekers that a public announcement of more than one million of them could provoke. Consequently, the authorities drastically revised this figure downwards.

However, more than such statistical dispute, what really matters are the implications of this system. First, the actual need for protection from the South African state is not reflected in the status of asylum seeker, let alone of refugee, granted to claimants: an unknown, but certainly high, proportion of applicants become undocumented simply because of the complications of the procedure; conversely, many of them confess having left their country for economic rather than political reasons, although both elements are often closely related. In short, neither the legal categories, which differentiate asylum seekers from undocumented foreigners, nor the administrative criteria, which distinguish between migrants and refugees, seem empirically relevant. Second, the experience of the applicants is little influenced by the legal status they obtain: in fact, asylum seekers and undocumented foreigners are confronted with almost similar problems in terms of precarity, unemployment, illegal housing, hostility from nationals, and even repression by the state. In the end, their tribulations prove to be very similar: they beg or sell in the streets, and they rent a shack on a plot in the townships or squat in abandoned buildings of the city, while being under the constant threat of the police, gangs, and outbreaks of xenophobic violence.

Such was the case of the Zimbabwean women with whom I conducted an ethnographic research in Johannesburg in May and June 2013.[23] A group of them lived on the third floor of a five-story unlawfully occupied building in the Central Business District. The large surface was divided into approximately six-square-meter rooms by plywood and cardboard partition walls much lower than the high ceiling. Electric wires routed to illegal connections made a dense web overlooking the makeshift apartments. The sounds of conversations and radio broadcasts mixed in an indiscernible background noise of voices and music. One of the women I met, in her thirties, lived with her partner and their baby in one of these rooms, without any comfort or privacy. The broken window let cold air in. There were a bed, a table, a small cabinet, a heating plate, an old television set, and two upturned buckets on the cemented floor, used as rudimentary stools. The only decorations were three posters representing the Gaza Strip, the Rastafari religion, and an advertisement for a soft drink. The place was as decent as could be under the circumstances.

The young woman explained the context that had led her to leave her country: she was a member of the main opposition party and had been assaulted and beaten by a group of government supporters. Her family had advised her to flee; having hardly any resources to raise her first two children, she had handed them to her parents' care before her departure. During her first three years in South Africa, she had no documents. At some point, friends suggested that she apply for refugee status, which she did, but six months later, when she tried to renew her permit, she was told that she would have to pay a fee for being late, which she was unable to do. She had been undocumented again since then. Soliciting charity to survive, she was constantly bullied by law-enforcement officers, only avoiding arrests on various occasions because she suborned them or sometimes because they felt pity for her child. Staying in an abandoned building, she had also been exposed to frequent police raids but had managed to avoid being deported by bribing the officers at the police station. Remarkably and paradoxically, it was the very station where she had found refuge during the attacks targeting migrants that had made dozens of victims around the country. The same police officers who had mistreated her on numerous occasions had then protected her from the angry mob. Despite this growing adversity, she insisted that because of the terrible political and economic situation in Zimbabwe, there was no other option for her than to remain in South Africa. "It is hard to live here, but we have to cope with it," she concluded with a weary smile.

Although the dozens of stories of asylum seekers and undocumented foreigners that I collected in the dark buildings were always unique, similar themes kept coming back: in their homeland, a combination of persecution and poverty that forced them to leave; in their host country, bureaucratic malfunctioning and endemic corruption that rendered the perspective of refugee status illusory, while police harassment, multiple arrests, fear of deportation, risk of pogroms, lack of resources, and feelings of insecurity made the asylum they had hoped to find in South Africa merely a word.

Beyond the difference in historical and political contexts, the young Syrian men in Calais and the young Zimbabwean women in Johannesburg share a common form of life. It is the form of life of wandering strangers who have left the country of their citizenship because their very physical existence was under threat and who are maintained in an untenable legal and social precarity by the country in which they found refuge but where their rights are not recognized. In Calais, one calls them "migrants" or "refugees." The distinction between the two terms is indeed formally significant, and there is a fierce battle over the way to designate them since the authorities tend to use the term "migrants" to deny their claim to a right to protection while non-governmental organizations name them "refugees" to emphasize their entitlement to such right. Yet, beyond this lexical argument, they are actually undocumented individuals living in makeshift shelters and subjected to police brutality. In Johannesburg, one refers to them as "asylum seekers" or "illegal aliens." Again, there is a difference between the two, since those who have an asylum permit are in principle guaranteed certain rights, particularly regarding access to healthcare and to education for their children, from which those who are not in possession of such a document cannot benefit. Yet, whatever their legal status is, they all experience the same daily hardship from being exposed to destitution, state violence, and hostility from nationals.

The various legal categories distinguishing those forced by circumstances to leave their country and find refuge in another are therefore highly porous: not only do foreigners often move from one category to another along the administrative process, but also, even when they do not, the representation that others as well as themselves have of their status changes depending on context. A man traveling across France is more likely to be considered a refugee if he is an Eritrean than if he is a Nigerian, but, once in Calais, he will regardless be treated as an unwelcome migrant who will be prevented from getting into England by all possible means. In the event that he finally decides to claim the protection of the French government, which exceptionally occurs, he will become an asylum seeker for several months before being rejected in six cases out of ten if he is Eritrean and nine out of ten if he is Nigerian. He will then become an undocumented foreigner exposed to the risk of being deported. Similarly, in South Africa, as any Mozambican or Congolese woman is well aware of, non-nationals are more easily identified through their appearance and their accent than by their documents, and whether their status is that of asylum seekers or undocumented migrants, they almost always end up in low-quality, often illegal dwellings, only finding resources in the informal – sometimes illicit – sector of the economy, and becoming the victims of police harassment and possible pogroms. Legal categories are therefore simultaneously important and insignificant: they either define a status or reject outside of the law, with obvious consequences in terms of positive and negative rights, but they do not make any major differences in the way those concerned are viewed and treated in their everyday life by state agents as well as the general public. In fact, these men and women often do not know themselves what their legal status or lack thereof actually is.

But why is the concept of form of life relevant to account for the configuration that characterizes refugees and migrants in the jungle of Calais, or the asylum seekers and undocumented foreigners in the dark buildings of Johannesburg? Indeed, it is not sufficient to establish what they have in common, as I have done so far. It is also necessary to justify the recourse to this concept through which one can grasp their presence to the world. I propose to do so on the basis of the discussion I have undertaken with the works of Wittgenstein, Canguilhem, and Agamben. Forced nomadism, which leads these men and women to live, sometimes with their children, in limbo at the margins of society and the state, involves a threefold dialectical relation. First, this condition illustrates the interplay between the universal and the particular. Whatever the exact circumstances that led to their departure, often a combination of danger, poverty, and hope, and whatever the legal and political context of the country where they sought refuge, all these exiles face similar uncertainty about their status and vulnerability regarding their position. Yet each group, with its history, its culture, and its environment, has a singular experience, which is both immediately intelligible to all its members and largely incommunicable to others. Think, for instance, of how comparable as well as unique are, in their respective camps in Italy, the experiences of marginality lived through by Roma people just arrived from Romania and Bulgaria and by African migrants, survivors of the crossing of the Mediterranean Sea. Second, this situation emphasizes the tension between the biological and the biographical. For these exiles, the question of survival is primarily physical, with the priority being given to obtaining food, shelter, and minimal security. But these elementary needs can only be satisfied as part of a trajectory, in the course of which relationships with other agents are built, be they aid workers offering their assistance or police officers preventing access to resources. In this respect, enclosing refugees behind fences and throwing bags of food over the barbed wire, as in Hungary, or settling them in reception centers and providing them with moral and material support, as in Germany, traces a crucial line between treating persons as animals or humans. Third, this situation reveals the complex interaction between law and practice. The legal status determines the right to stay on the territory of the host country and even to expect some benefits, but those who do not hold this right quickly learn how to circumvent or at least accommodate to legal obstacles. Indeed, rules are decided by the authorities and imposed on foreigners, although with considerable differences in terms of aggressiveness or, conversely, benevolence from one country or one period to another. Yet, refugees and migrants manage to maintain a certain margin of liberty through which they can deploy tactics and play with the rules. Even in the most extreme circumstances, refugees and migrants find solutions to the problems they face, negotiate arrangements with local agents, develop solidarities, imagine futures – and strive to rebuild a normal form of life. In the three dimensions explored, the form of life of forced nomads therefore proceeds from the application of both constraints and possibilities, among those who are in charge of these situations as well as those who are affected by them.

What the concept of form of life thus brings to light in a unique manner – and the reason why it is essential to reflect on these human experiences – stems from these three dialectical relations. But it does more.

On the one hand, the concept allows us to rethink the vulnerability that Sandra Laugier describes as that "which people feel when they try, on a daily basis, to embody their subjectivity and explore ways of being human, and which tragically appears in situations of loss of the ordinary life," this reading allowing her to connect forms of life and care.[24] In light of the research on forced nomads, however, we can formulate two observations. First, vulnerability is not just a matter of subjectivity; it also results from an objective situation which is simultaneously material, legal, and social. Second, the tragic does not only occur as a result of the loss of the ordinary life, but it can also be inscribed in the ordinary life itself. Therefore, there is a dual tension: structural, between the subjective and the objective; temporal, between the event and the permanent.

On the other hand, the concept provides us with the possibility of revisiting the notion of precariousness, which for Judith Butler is "based upon an understanding of how easily human life is annulled" in contexts of violence and war.[25] The case of forced nomads suggests yet again two remarks. First, it is important to distinguish precariousness as a universal experience of the finitude and therefore fragility of human existence, and precarity as the condition of those exposed to the inequality, discrimination, injustice, or persecution that threaten this existence. The former is underpinned by the universal biological limit of the living, and the latter by social inequalities in life. Second, since the word comes from legal Latin *precarius*, which means "what is obtained through prayer," there remains in the adjective "precarious" something of the original idea of favor being granted, and therefore of dependence on whoever has the power to grant it, starting with the state, an idea that only the second meaning retains. Consequently, it is crucial to distinguish the two senses, to avoid subsuming the political under the ethical. All lives are precarious but certain lives much more so than others – and, above all, quite differently. Here again a dual tension can be found: social, because of the inequality of lives, and relational, in the subjection instituted.

Needless to say, forced nomadism does not constitute the only vulnerable and precarious form of life in terms of transnational circulation of human beings; it could interestingly be contrasted with the form of life experienced by temporary migrant workers inserted in the global capitalist market with particularly restrictive contracts, as is the case for Filipinas doing domestic work in the United Arab Emirates, or with no contract at all, as is the case for Mexicans working in farms located in the United States during harvest season.[26] On the one hand, this form of life also involves a tension between the universal and the particular, tests the biological body and the biographical trajectory, and depends on the rigor of the law while being adjusted in practice. But, on the other hand, the parallel between migrant workers and forced nomads would highlight the difference between the two forms of life, as in the first case the workforce, exploited and captive, is regarded as necessary to the economy, whereas, in the second one, the unwelcome migrants are deemed useless, being alternatively an object of sympathy and exclusion.

The idea of form of life has emerged from distinct – and some would say incompatible – philosophical traditions for which, moreover, contradictory interpretations often exist among exegetes. Most authors thus opt for one tradition and one interpretation, usually ignoring theoretical alternatives. In my discussion of Wittgenstein, Canguilhem, and Agamben, I have aimed to follow a different path, not by trying to reconcile these approaches, but rather by discussing them dialectically. The tensions resulting from this confrontation – between universal and particular, biology and biography, law and practice – provided three lines of force to rethink collective human experiences that, albeit distant in time and space, can be conceived of as similar forms of life.

To demonstrate the heuristic import of the concept thus reformulated, I have taken the example of the forced nomadic form of life. It is that of dozens of millions of people on the five continents, whether they are considered undocumented aliens or asylum seekers, economic migrants or refugees. The vast majority of them are in Africa, Asia, and the Middle East, and not in Western countries as we are led to believe. Guatemalans in the United States, Bolivians in Argentina, Afghans in Australia, Rohingyas in Bangladesh, Somalis in Egypt, Sudanese in Kenya, Syrians in Turkey, Palestinians in Lebanon, Roma people across Europe, to name a few, they are literally innumerable. Limiting the count to those deemed "forcibly displaced as a result of persecution, conflict, generalized violence, or human rights violations," in the language of the United Nations High Commissioner for Refugees, their number amounted to 70 million in 2016 – including 5 million Palestinian refugees, who depend on a distinct institution – of which approximately a third are out of their own country.[27] These statistics do not include, however, all those who share a comparable fate due to poverty, catastrophes, and climatic disasters. Whatever their specific history, forced nomads, whose existence is under threat in their home country, are generally unwanted in the nations where they have sought refuge. They have to face the contradictions of policies that oscillate between rejection and protection, brutal repression and mere indifference, indefinite detention and humanitarian assistance, denial of regularization and recognition of rights. They sought security and end up in wastelands or abandoned buildings, sometimes prisons or camps. Still, they often consider their current condition a little less desperate than their previous one.

To speak of the form of life of these men, women, and children deprived of a home country and undesirable in their host country is to account for shared human experiences as well as specific cultural contexts, exposure to physical threats as well as social endangerment, legal uncertainties as well as pragmatic arrangements. But the constraints these forms of life entail do not exhaust their reality. As suggested in Robert Musil's epigraph, under the surface of what appears to irremediably impose itself on individuals, imagination and energy manifest themselves, expectations and desires are expressed. Under the form, life remains.

However, it is necessary to push the analysis further. The form of life of forced nomads does not only describe their condition. It also tells of a certain state of the world. Indeed, this form of life results from the predicament of contemporary democracies, incapable of living up to the principles that constitute the foundation of their very existence. The conjunction of massive displacements of populations fleeing conflicts, disasters, and poverty, and of no less impressive reactions of hostility fueled by populist rhetoric, is a signature of our time. Yet a pitfall must be avoided: presentism. Since the beginning of the twentieth century, Europe has gone through several periods of considerable demographic movements, which have often generated reactions of xenophobia: in the 1920s, after the Russian Revolution and World War I, leading to the creation of the International Office for Refugees; in the late 1940s, after World War II, precipitating the ratification of the Convention Relating to the Status of Refugees.[28] The parallel between these tragic moments and the contemporary crisis is too easily eluded by those who see the present time as exceptional in this respect.

In a short article published in 1943, Hannah Arendt illustrates in the first person the experience of this form of life: "We were expelled from Germany because we were Jews. But having hardly crossed the French borderline, we were changed into 'boches' ... At the beginning of the war we were interned ... all the same."[29] Such was also Walter Benjamin's fate after his departure from Nazi Germany. Having found a temporary haven in Paris, he was imprisoned in a French camp at the beginning of World War II. Liberated thanks to his friends' intervention with the authorities, he had to flee further south as the German forces invaded France. Having obtained a visa for the United States with Max Horkheimer's assistance, he headed for Spain, undertook an exhausting clandestine hike across the Pyrenees, and finally arrived in Portbou on the other side of the border, only to be arrested by the Spanish police who told him that he would be sent back to France. It is in the hotel room where he was confined until his transfer that he died after having taken a high dose of morphine, a gesture the interpretation of which remains debated. In the manuscript that he was putatively keeping preciously in his suitcase during his gruesome journey, *Theses on the Philosophy of History*, he had written: "The current amazement that the things we are experiencing are 'still' possible in the twentieth century is not philosophical. This amazement is not the beginning of knowledge – unless it is the knowledge that the view of history which gives rise to it is untenable."[30] Pursuing his visionary reflection, Benjamin interpreted Paul Klee's famous drawing *Angelus Novus* that he had purchased two decades earlier. He imagined it as the "angel of history" whose "face is turned toward the past," where the "chain of events" appears to him as "one single catastrophe which keeps piling wreckage upon wreckage." It is certainly disturbing that some of the "events" which he faced then would be " 'still' possible" in the beginning of the twenty-first century, dooming his "angel of history" to contemplate again and again the same forms of life that these tragic events produce.

II
Ethics of Life

I say: Life defined only as the opposite of death is not life.

Mahmoud Darwish, *Almond Blossoms
and Beyond*, 2009

What characterizes a good life? How should one conduct oneself in order to live such a good life? The awareness of the finitude of their existence has long led human beings to reflect on the meaning of life, and in particular on its moral meaning. This reflection, which has nourished philosophy at least since Plato, was developed through various ethical approaches to what is good, just, important to do with one's life, and suitable to do with the life of others. Such inquiry is certainly inseparable from that on forms of life. Indeed, since it is empirically established that the responses to these ethical questions vary from one place to another, from one period to another, even from one person to another, theory has to determine whether universal normative foundations exist, possibly inscribed in the neuronal circuits, as cognitivists believe, or whether morality is always culturally circumscribed, temporally situated, and even dependent on circumstances, as ethnologists and historians show.

Having long made the study of remote societies characterized by distinct sets of norms and values their hallmark, while insistently affirming their intention to apprehend the unity of mankind for epistemological as much as political reasons, anthropologists have significantly contributed to this reflection. Their positioning has generally oscillated between a benevolent relativism, which simultaneously served to acknowledge the culture of others and criticize the claim to superiority of their own culture, and a critical engagement, which ranged from the condemnation of local practices to the denunciation of flaws in their own society. In fact, over the last decades, the growing concern over ethics manifested within the discipline, not only in the practice of ethnography but also as a matter to investigate, can be read in part as an attempt to respond to this ambiguous positioning.

Pursuing the dialogue between philosophy and anthropology, I propose to analyze the terms of the theoretical discussion, which, in both disciplines, confront two opposite views whereby ethical lives are, for some, defined by principles external to individuals, whether these principles are universal or local, and, for others, produced through internal processes of self-realization, whether these processes are subjective or intersubjective. Beyond their divergences, these approaches tend to devise an ethical substance, already there or in the making, that can be isolated from its historical construction, social inscription, and political implications. Yet, from the moment one leaves the realm of philosophical abstractions to examine ethics in concrete situations, it is difficult to ignore this threefold dimension of the historical, the social, and the political. Such is particularly the case if one operates a conceptual shift consisting in moving from a normative study of ethical life to a critical analysis of the ethics of life, in other words from an interrogation on what a good life is to a questioning of the way life has become the supreme good in contemporary societies. In this perspective, I will propose two case studies, on the regularization of foreigners suffering from severe ailment in France and on the treatment of individuals living with AIDS in South Africa, so as to bring to light the tension between two aspects, one social and political, the other physical and biological, the latter tending today to prevail more and more often over the former. However, the new balance finds itself compromised when tested in tragic contexts, as I will demonstrate through a study on the Israeli–Palestinian conflict in which it is a matter of saving the lives of others, for humanitarians, and of sacrificing their own lives to defend their cause, for resistant fighters in the Occupied Territories. It will thus become clear that there exist different ethics of life.

Having scrupulously avoided the subject during his entire life, Michel Foucault devoted to the moral question several of his last writings, which two decades later have become the source of a renaissance of moral anthropology. Indeed, for a long time, he had kept away from this question, under the influence of both Nietzsche, which he claimed, and Marx, which he denied, inheriting from the former the questioning of its Judeo-Christian foundation and from the latter the denunciation of its bourgeois origin. Besides, his own intellectual project, as he had developed it during his archeological period, implied a criticism of the constitution of a modern subject in which morality appeared to be a set of conventions imposed on individuals through games of power and knowledge. He was therefore as far from a moral philosophy as could be, and for reasons that were not completely foreign to those which also rendered the founders of the Frankfurt School suspicious of it. Significantly, in the series of essays Max Horkheimer had gathered for a republication in English in a collection entitled *Critical Theory*, he had renounced featuring the article "Materialismus und Moral," indicating that one should publish only what one is ready to support without any reservation, thereby revealing the discomfort felt by him and his colleagues toward moral philosophy.[1] But as far as Foucault was concerned, it was not just morality that he viewed as problematic: it was any sort of topic that could evoke a free sovereign agent, and furthermore, it was any sort of normative thinking, which for him could only be the expression of a moral authority. This is precisely what Jürgen Habermas reproached him for in the famous debate that opposed the two philosophers: the lack of normative foundations, or rather what he considered to be a sort of denial, by Foucault, of his own "cryptonormative" positions.[2] Whatever one thinks of this criticism, it is clear that it does not apply to the French philosopher's last works.

Indeed, in the eight years that separate the publication of the first volume of *The History of Sexuality* from that of the second and third, a radical inflexion occurs in Foucault's intellectual trajectory: it is often designated as his "ethical turn." The last three lectures at the Collège de France, from that on the "hermeneutics of the subject" onwards, are particularly significant in that regard. But it is in the brief text "Morality and the Practice of the Self" that he offers the most systematic and condensed formulation.[3] There are three ways of considering morality, Foucault writes: as a "moral code," that is, "a set of values and rules of action that are recommended to individuals through the intermediary of various prescriptive agencies," such as family, school, and churches; as "the morality of behaviors," namely "the manner in which they comply more or less fully with a standard of conduct, the manner in which they obey or resist an interdiction or a prescription," thus indicating both adherence to and transgression of rules; finally, as the formation of a "moral subject," corresponding to the "manner in which one ought to 'conduct oneself'," or more precisely "the manner in which one ought to form oneself as a moral subject," through the experience of conducting one's conduct. In fact, Foucault later reduces this triptych into a simple diptych with, on the one hand, "codes of behavior," moral norms that society or the group imposes on individuals, and, on the other hand, "forms of subjectivation," the moral becoming of subjects through the exercise of their freedom to act ethically. However, the two dimensions are not exclusive: one can find within medieval Christianity " 'code-oriented'

moralities" and " 'ethics-oriented' moralities," among which
"there have been, at different times, juxtapositions, rival-
ries and conflicts, and compromises." It is clearly in the
latter approach that Foucault is interested, both intellectu-
ally and personally.

However, the dualism he identifies is anything but new:
it is inscribed in the long history of philosophy. On the one
hand, the idea of categorical imperatives defining morality
is at the heart of Kant's duty ethics, which gives individuals
obligations to comply with. On the other hand, the notion
of personal dispositions guiding individuals toward a good
life is the essence of Aristotle's virtue ethics, according to
which individuals establish the right way to conduct themselves. These two ethics constitute, with consequential-
ism, the triptych of Western normative moral philosophy.
Significantly, they also form the basis of the approach to
morality in anthropology.[4] Indeed, under the influence of
Émile Durkheim's study of moral facts, duty ethics has
long been the quasi-exclusive reference for the rare works
on morality, which aimed to describe and interpret the
moral norms in a given society. But with the recent interest
in Foucault's last writings on moral subjectivities, the field
has gone through a major change, the ambition being now
to account for the formation of ethical subjects through
the exercise of their free will or simply through their ordinary practices. The first line of research is often described
as anthropology of morality; the second as anthropology
of ethics.

Although death interrupted Durkheim's grand project
dedicated to morality, some of his late writings incorporate
his vision of it. He explicitly follows Kant's ethics with the
exception that, in line with his sociological thinking, he
asserts his will to strip this ethics of its normative dimension and affirms that he wants to "explore and understand"
what he calls "moral reality" rather than "evaluate it."[5]
Furthermore, while he considers that "morality appears to
us as a system of rules of conduct," in which the "obligation is, then, one of the primary characteristics of the

moral rule," he adds that "the notion of duty does not exhaust the concept of morality." For us to act morally, it is not enough that we feel constrained to do so by a rule imposed by society: this act must also "appear to us as, in some way, desirable," this second characteristic being "no less important than the first." Thus, in Durkheim's view, morality is duty plus desire. Where does its founding principle reside? Not in individuals, since they can never be an "end" to their own moral conduct but in the group: "society is the end of all moral activity," and "morality begins with life in the group." Morality is therefore consubstantial to society. In this vein, from Edward Westermarck's 1906 monumental cross-cultural catalogue of "moral ideas" to Signe Howell's 1997 eclectic collection of case studies on "local moralities," anthropologists have endeavored to establish the "moral codes" of various societies and groups, that is, the set of rules, norms, and values to which they adhere and the violation of which would subject them to punishment.[6] Interesting enrichments of this approach have been proposed by taking into account emotions in the practice of morality, as in Lila Abu-Lughod's ethnography of Egyptian Bedouin women, and by paying attention to conflicts between moralities of distinct traditions, as in Joel Robbins's study of Christian native people of Papua New Guinea.[7] Long dominant, this approach to morality, which emphasizes its collective and imposed dimension, has been recently challenged.

Indeed, with Foucault's last writings, a completely new perspective on the moral subject is opened. The keys to these "practices of the self," through which individuals transform themselves, are to be found in ancient Greek philosophy. For instance, *enkrateia*, which "is characterized more by an active form of self-mastery, which enables one to resist or struggle, and to achieve domination in the area of desires and pleasures," is to be distinguished from the *sōphrosunē*, through which "the subject deliberately chooses reasonable principles of action, that he is capable of following and that he holds to the 'right mean' between

insensitivity and excess."[8] These moral exercises thus
proceed from an Aristotelian ethics in which various
virtues are mobilized. But they exceed it to a certain extent
as virtuous actions are inscribed in a larger project of
moral subjectivation. In that regard, one could speak of a
genuine "ethical work that one performs on oneself, not
only in order to bring one's conduct into compliance with
a given rule, but to attempt to transform oneself into the
ethical subject of one's behavior." According to Foucault,
ethics has thus no foundation, whether metaphysical or
psychological as in metaethics, nor does it have standards,
whether duty, consequences, or virtues. It is self-contained
in the formation of a moral subject. This approach has
exercised a profound influence on anthropology, from
Talal Asad's research on discipline in the Christian monastic world to James Faubion's study of a millenarian sect,
while Jarrett Zigon and James Laidlaw have put Foucault's
reading of ethics in dialogue with Martin Heidegger's and
Alasdair MacIntyre's, respectively.[9] But Foucault is no
more the only philosopher whose works underlie the flour-
ishing field of the anthropology of ethics than religion is
the only domain in which ethical practices can be ethno-
graphically attested. What Veena Das and Michael Lambek
call "ordinary ethics" has been the subject of seminal
research, in India for the former and Mayotte for the latter,
based on a reflection inspired by the philosophies of language developed by Wittgenstein and Austin: their project
is both epistemological and ethical as they want to acknowledge and rehabilitate the ethics at work in people's everyday life.[10] Beyond the variety of influences they proceed
from and of theories they propose, all these approaches
have in common the aim of looking at ethics as a sort of
fulfillment of agents' lives, either through religious engagements or through mundane acts.

A simplified but fairly correct depiction of the anthropological landscape can thus delineate an anthropology of
moral systems, mostly interested in the social codes that
guide conducts, and an anthropology of ethical subjects,

mainly focused on the process of self-realization of individuals. However distinct they may be, the two paradigms tend to share a common theoretical and methodological assumption: as a gem can be extracted from its gangue, morality or ethics can be extricated and purified by analysis, either as a moral substance or as an ethical process. For Durkheim and his followers, the paradoxical claim is simultaneously that morality can be understood as a unique system of specific rules and that society is the moral authority governing these rules, in other words, that morality is part of the society while being coextensive to it. For Foucault and his disciples, the hermeneutics of the subject disconnects the reflexive exercise of creating a moral self from its social conditions of possibility, even though from its origins in ancient Greece it has always been determined by inequalities of status, gender, and origin. Thus, in the first case, morality resides in society, while in the other, ethics proceeds from the subject. But in both, morality and ethics seem to be separable from the historical background, the social structure, and the political domain.

To account for these three dimensions, I preferred to speak, in my own work, of moral questions and ethical stakes, in other words, of facts which do not suppose preexisting morality or ethics but are produced by agents in a particular context.[11] Morality and ethics never appear as pure objects, but as realities permeated by the historical, social, and political contexts in which they are formed. In this regard, of the three versions of normative moral philosophy, consequentialist ethics is the only one with hardly any anthropological posterity, but also the only one to offer an impure vision of morality, since judging an act by its foreseeable effects necessarily involves having to take into account other dimensions of social life. This is what Max Weber was pleading for when he contrasted the pragmatic approach of the ethics of responsibility to the categorical nature of the ethics of conviction.[12] And it is in the name of the former that he opposed the 1918 uprisings when protagonists epitomized the latter.

Thus, if one strictly follows the two dominant paradigms of moral anthropology, which stem from two of the
three normative moral philosophies, a deep tension appears
regarding what could be called "ethical life."[13] Is it defined
according to local reasoning, which translates into the
moral codes every society, even group, dictates, or according to universal principles, determining the ideals toward
which moral subjects strive to tend? Is this dilemma of
ethical life unsolvable? Axel Honneth addresses this question at the end of *The Struggle for Recognition*.[14] Indeed,
he proposes to resolve the contradiction between the idea
that morality lies within universal principles that impose
themselves on ethical life and the idea that morality
depends on particular historical conditions according to
which ethical life is determined. In the first approach,
ethical life is devalued since it is merely subordinated to
universal principles, while in the second approach, morality is relativized because it varies from one place or one
period to another. In an effort to move beyond this tension,
Honneth asserts that "the structural elements" of ethical
life "can be normatively extracted" from "the plurality of
all particular forms of life." To the individual autonomy
defended by Kant, for whom human beings should always
be viewed as ends in themselves, one should prefer the
intersubjective conditions argued for by Hegel, according
to whom they fulfill themselves through the recognition of
others. Indeed, this "experience of recognition" enables
self-confidence, self-respect, and self-esteem, which constitute the three components of self-realization through interaction with others. Such experience is foundational, as
Honneth later exposes in his debate with Nancy Fraser,
since it is through the struggle for recognition that one can
pose the question of redistribution, and therefore, ultimately, of social justice, and not the reverse.[15] As proof of
it, he emphasizes the fact that, in the history of social
movements, the issue of trampled dignity generally precedes the demand for better material conditions. This
Hegelian approach to ethical life, as Honneth develops it,

is of interest as it fills a gap in the sociological analysis and restores the antagonistic nature of the social world: on the one hand, the emphasis on the intersubjective dimension provides the missing link between the societal level of moral codes and the individual level of moral subjects; on the other hand, the importance granted to mobilizations reintegrates the conflictive aspect of social relations which studies on morality and ethics tend to overlook.

This brief evocation of moral philosophies and anthropologies shows that ethics – whether approached through Kant or Aristotle, Durkheim or Foucault, whether considered from a perspective that is universalist or relativist, individual or intersubjective – essentially aims to determine what is a good life and how one should endeavor to lead such a life. But there is another question, more rarely posed, regarding the value given to life and the way contemporary societies came to consider it to be the supreme good. This is the question I am interested in and, to distinguish the answers I am trying to provide, I will substitute the concept of ethics of life for that of ethical life. Such a reformulation of the relation between ethics and life proceeds from an approach similar to Nietzsche's with regard to morality. He writes: "Even then my real concern was something much more important than hypothesis-mongering, whether my own or other people's, on the origin of morality ... What was at stake was the *value* of morality."[16] Indeed, what is at stake in the reversal of perspective that I propose is the value of life in terms of its ethical and political implications. I will analyze both, first through the condition of people suffering from life-threatening diseases, then through the tension existing between the saving of others' lives and the sacrifice of one's life.

Like the rest of Western Europe, France began closing its borders to migrants in the mid-1970s as the result of specific circumstances, namely the oil crisis and the subsequent economic recession, and structural changes, such as the mechanization of the industry leading to a drastic reduction in the need for an unskilled workforce.[17] These restrictions were initially limited to labor migration but were soon extended to family reunification and later to most situations that had, until then, given foreigners a right to reside. Even people who had lived in France for years were affected by the political change as the authorities could refuse the renewal of their residence permits, alleging a national preference in the corresponding branch. Although their condition pertained to an entirely distinct philosophy defined by international conventions, asylum seekers were also concerned by this policy as it was commonly argued that many among them were actually economic migrants trying to take advantage of the international protection for victims of persecution. Within three decades the admission rate to refugee status dropped from more than 90 percent to less than 10 percent.

In this context, in which all doors were closing inexorably on legal immigration of any sort, there was a remarkable exception. The "humanitarian rationale," as it was officially termed, concerned undocumented migrants whose life was endangered by a serious health issue for which treatment was not accessible in their home country.[18] It entitled them, on the basis of certification by a physician and validation by the authorities, to a temporary residence permit and to medical care. The recognition of this right had been the result of a long campaign led by human rights and humanitarian non-governmental organizations. Fiercely negotiated, it had gone through progressive steps with initially a discretionary power granted to the local state representative, then a limited guarantee not to be deported but without possibility of being regularized, and finally an extensive right to temporary residence with permission to work and free access to healthcare. The procedure was an immediate success and soon became the most frequent modality for undocumented immigrants to obtain papers. In 1997, the year after the law was passed, 455 persons had benefited from it. In 2005, this number skyrocketed, with 7,737 beneficiaries. It represented a 17-fold increase in less than a decade. That same year the French Office for the Protection of Refugees and Stateless People granted asylum to only 4,184 claimants while a record number of 55,678 were rejected.[19] The admission rate was then 60 percent for first-time applicants invoking the humanitarian rationale but only 8 percent for claimants to refugee status in the first instance. The chance of being regularized was thus seven times higher when one's life was threatened by the existence of a disease rather than by a risk of persecution. Of course, in the first case, the administration could rely on a medical certificate whereas, in the second case, it had to trust the claimant's word – which was manifestly not enough any more.

One case will illustrate what this evolution of the moral attitude toward immigration and asylum concretely meant for those concerned. It is that of a young Haitian woman who came to France in the early 1990s. The account she gave me was tragically banal. During the political instability that marked the decade following the 1991 military coup in Haiti, her father, a political opponent to the regime, was murdered by unknown assailants and, a few months later, her mother in turn disappeared. One day, when the young woman was at home with her boyfriend, several men burst into her house and gang-raped her. In the context of insecurity at the time, she did not know whether this was a targeted operation or a random assault. After a short stay at her aunt's to try to recover from the trauma, she made the decision to leave the country and seek asylum in France, as did many of her compatriots: Haitians were then the third most numerous applicants to refugee status, but their admission rate was one of the lowest, only 3.3 percent in the first instance, reaching 7.1 percent after appeal.[20] As was the case for almost all the claimants from her country, she was denied asylum. Having become undocumented, she hid at her brother's place, not daring to go out for fear of being arrested and deported. At some point, however, her physical and mental health deteriorated and her partner, who was in a similar legal limbo, took her to the hospital, where she was diagnosed with full-blown AIDS. A probable consequence of the sexual assault of which she had been the victim, the infection attested in retrospect to the truthfulness of her account. This time, she applied for regularization using the humanitarian rationale procedure. She was almost immediately granted temporary documents as was the case for more than 90 percent of people living with AIDS at the time.[21] Her health status rapidly improved by means of the treatment administered at the hospital. A few weeks later, she went back to her brother's place with a residence permit and antiretroviral drugs.

During that period, in France, it was not rare for asylum seekers whose claim had been rejected to be asked by their counsel, by the human rights activists who assisted them, or even by well-intentioned state bureaucrats in the immigration office whether they did not suffer from a disease that could justify the claim to a regularization through the humanitarian rationale procedure. Such was rarely the case and, paradoxically, a sort of shared disappointment was then perceptible among the migrants and their helpers as they realized that this ultimate option too was debarred, although it meant that the person did not have a life-threatening condition. An undocumented Nigerian engineer who had stayed in Germany and later France at the end of his studies was quite aware of this strange relation between health status and residency rights. Having eventually been granted a temporary permit after the discovery of an HIV infection at an advanced stage, and knowing that he owed his precarious legal status to his compromised medical condition, he sadly commented to me: "This disease that kills me is also what allows me to live."

The inverse slopes of the curves of regularization in relation to the humanitarian rationale and to the right to asylum thus reveal a distinction that was implicitly established in the last decade of the twentieth century between two ways of considering life. This distinction plays at two levels: the vital threat and the evidence of it. In terms of threat, asylum responds to a political peril whereas human-itarianism supposes a pathological menace. In terms of evidence, officers and judges search for biographical elements justifying state protection while physicians look for biological proofs securing a diagnosis. The decrease in admission rates for asylum seekers reflects the declining legitimacy of the political threat and its biographical evidence: officers and judges now even expect medical or psychological certificates attesting to the persecution endured in the form of corporeal scars or psychic trauma. Conversely, the increase in regularization numbers for sick migrants reveals the rising legitimacy of the pathological threat and its biological evidence: the latter is viewed as more empirically robust and the former as a more immediate source of concern. However, there might be more to it. Indeed, a disease seems both objective and value-free: it resides in the cells and the organs. On the contrary, persecution implies taking the side of victims and delivering value judgments: it is about causes and ideologies. The institutions of the host countries feel more comfortable with the supposed neutrality of the former than with the suspected partiality of the latter.

This corresponds to a recent change in the moral evaluation of asylum seekers and undocumented foreigners. In the 1970s, Chileans fleeing the Pinochet dictatorship were much more welcome than Chechens trying to escape the Kadyrov regime in the 2000s, and the important mobilization of government authorities to come to the rescue, in the South China Sea, of the boat people fleeing communist repression in Vietnam contrasts with their timid reaction toward shipwrecks in the Mediterranean Sea, which concern victims of war, political violence, and endemic poverty in Africa. Symmetrically, until the 1970s, the diseased or disabled body of the immigrant symbolized the loss of its social value, as its presence could only be justified as labor force, and one even spoke of "sinistrosis" to refer pejoratively to the consequences of occupational hazards, whereas from the 1990s, the same impairment of physical integrity became an argument for regularization. A shift has therefore occurred in the ethics of life. The value of life as a social and political phenomenon has declined while its value as a natural and biological one has progressed. For those seeking to obtain a residence permit, an account of the persecution they face is now worth less than an HIV-positive test ...

This tension between the two forms of recognition of life was also at stake in a very different context: that of South Africa at the beginning of the twenty-first century. The AIDS epidemic, which had seemed, until then, to spare the country while it raged throughout the whole continent, soared in unprecedented proportions.[22] In the early 2000s, one in every eight HIV-positive persons in the world was South African, and one in every four pregnant women in South Africa was infected by the virus. Alarmist demographic projections anticipated a decline of 20 years in the life expectancy at birth within only two decades, a forecast that was later specified as regarding exclusively the black population, which rendered it even more dreadful.[23] With millions of individuals at risk of dying in the short term for lack of available treatment, it was the very diversity and even existence of the "rainbow nation" that seemed threatened, the most pessimistic predictions raising the specter of a depopulated country in which blacks would have become a minority. This situation was all the more dismaying since the country had just succeeded, against all expectations, in peacefully transitioning from apartheid to democracy. For many, South Africa seemed to be doomed to everlasting affliction, as it had just emerged from a terrible historical ordeal only to be confronted with an even more harrowing adversity. Moreover, this epidemiological crisis was intensified by an epistemological crisis. The head of state and his successive health ministers had indeed made infelicitous statements expressing their doubts about the viral origin of the epidemic and criticizing the efficacy as well as the innocuousness of antiretroviral drugs. They regarded poverty as the main reason for the rapid expansion of the disease and demanded that more clinical trials be conducted before expanding the use of the recently introduced medications. Inspired by Western scientists who had contested for more than a decade the widely accepted interpretation of the epidemic and the well-established benefits of the treatment, these dissident theses thrived on conspiracy theories, which echoed some of the revelations of the Truth and Reconciliation Commission. Indeed, it was discovered during the hearings that plots had been hatched by white supremacist groups as part of a so-called chemical and biological warfare, which included the injection of HIV to black prostitutes with the intention of contaminating the population of the townships. Soon the public sphere became intensely conflictive. On one side, the authorities accused the pharmaceutical industry of using African patients as "guinea pigs for the rest of the world." On the other side, activists blamed the government for letting them die by not providing any treatment; some were even speaking of a "Holocaust against the poor." Yet such dramatization eclipsed deeper truths.

These truths were brought to light during a debate I attended at the Witwatersrand University in Johannesburg, at the height of the controversy. Two well-known personalities of the fight against AIDS took the floor one after the other. The first one was the charismatic president of the Treatment Action Campaign, an activist organization advocating for access to antiretroviral drugs that had filed lawsuits against the government using the 1996 Constitution Bill of Rights, which stipulates that "everyone has the right to life." At the end of his inflammatory speech, in which he lashed out at the Health Department, he told the story of a woman who had recently died of AIDS, leaving behind three children who had been infected by the virus at birth, and concluded that he considered that health officials were "accomplices in the death of these children." As it happens, the second speaker was the director of the National AIDS Program, a woman who had never expressed sympathy for dissident theories and had the reputation of being a committed civil servant. Carefully distancing herself from the president's and minister's heterodox ideas, but reminding the audience of what the shift from an inferiority status to equal rights had meant for her and the majority of South Africans, she acknowledged the difficulties her position entailed due to "the legacy of the previous regime," in terms of racial segregation within the healthcare system, desperate shortage of economic resources and lack of competent personnel. Visibly hurt by the accusations thrown at her, she explained that she had to arbitrate on a daily basis between multiple demands under serious constraints, which notably implied "the major challenge of having to select" which problems to prioritize and which patients to treat. She described the painful dilemmas she faced when having to decide on such matters and affirmed that her main concern was to take into account the country's structural inequalities. "It is a question of equity," she added, before leaving the amphitheater holding back her tears.

Much more than the spectacular disputes on the controversies enjoyed and even fueled by the media, the exchange of views between the activist and the director revealed what I regard as the fundamental issue at stake for those confronted with the tragic expansion of the disease: it was not truth versus error, as was generally said, but the conflict between two truths; not ethic versus immorality, which was condemned, but the confrontation of two ethics. On one side, for activists and physicians, the central assertion was that each life counts. Newspapers were full of stories of patients who were said to be dying for lack of antiretroviral drugs and of images of babies who would allegedly not have been infected by the virus had their mother received preventive treatment when giving birth. The difficulties of implementation, the limited efficacy of the medications and their dangerous side effects, and the problems to reach patients who were often isolated or did not even know they were infected by the virus were underplayed. On the other side, public health and social development experts pointed out the shortcomings of the system, which exposed patients to defective surveillance, serious iatrogenic incidents, and above all major disparities in the distribution of the clinical benefits, while basic needs in terms of nutrition or housing were not met. Attuned to the historical conditions of a country still deeply affected by decades of apartheid, they worried about the measures adopted, which were likely to aggravate healthcare inequalities. In their reasoning, public good came before individual benefits.

Thus, the ultimate imperative was, for some, the affirmation of the value of each life and, for others, the defense of the equality of all lives. Not that the leader of the Treatment Action Campaign was indifferent to social justice: he had put his own life at play by refusing to take antiretroviral drugs until their access could be guaranteed to all in public institutions. Not that the director of the National AIDS Program lacked compassion: she had described with emotion her battle as that of a mother and an obstetrician personally and professionally committed to children's quality of life. But two ethical postures were at play: one situated the single life saved above all other priorities; the other gave precedence to fairness in the allocation of goods for the whole population. The emphasis was on the individual and the biological in the first case, and on the collective and the social in the second one. In the end, the activists prevailed. Antiretroviral drugs were made available in the public system, to the great benefit of many patients, although access to treatment was unevenly distributed. In the meantime, according to national surveys, inequalities increased, a third of the black population living with less than two dollars a day and one in every four individuals suffering from hunger, particularly in rural areas.[24] But this reality generated much less national and international mobilization than AIDS had.

The French immigration and asylum policies and the South African debates around antiretroviral drugs and public health epitomize the existence of two approaches to life: one that puts forward the physical existence and the biological aspects related to it; the other that gives prominence to the social context and the political dimension it reveals. In *Homo Sacer*, Giorgio Agamben proposed a distinction between two meanings of the word "life" based on two words found in ancient Greek writings: "*zoē*, which expressed the simple fact of living common to all living beings," and "*bios*, which indicated the form or way of living proper to an individual or a group." He speaks of "bare life" in the first case and "qualified life" in the second.[25] Yet, as he specifies in a later publication, this distinction is heuristic only as long as it is regarded as a paradigm, and not as a realistic representation, and as long as it is understood that it does not depict the experience of individuals but the way they are treated by society. Too often, this theory has been literally interpreted as meaning that the life of the refugee or of the terminally ill patient could be assimilated to "bare life," and therefore be deprived of its social and political dimensions, an interpretation about which Agamben himself is not without ambiguity, despite his claims to the contrary. This is why, to the duality of the nouns *zoē* and *bios*, which lends itself to a certain essentialization, I prefer the complex interactions and permanent reconfigurations of the two pairs of adjectives physical/biological and social/political.

Interestingly, the two cases have two different temporalities: in the French policies, a succession of the two logics, with a shift from the political (asylum) to the biological (disease); conversely, in the South African debates, a concomitance, with a competition between the social (fairness) and the physical (treatment). But significantly, in both, it is the physical/biological that prevails over the social/political. This trend signals the rise of biolegitimacy, the legitimacy of life, that is, the recognition of life as a supreme good in the name of which any action can ultimately be justified.[26] The life in question is before anything else the physical and biological life as opposed to – and often to the detriment of – the social and political life. For the French state, the threat to the physical life of the diseased migrant seems more worthy of attention than the menace to the political life of the asylum seeker. In South African society, the risk for the biological life of the AIDS patient appears to be more intolerable than the perspective of inequities among the social lives of the poor. Analyzing the aftermath of the Chernobyl nuclear explosion, Adriana Petryna shows how it was only through their biological condition that the residents could exercise their social rights and only by proving health effects that they could fully become Ukrainian citizens. As she expresses it: "The damaged biology of a population has become the grounds for social membership and the basis for staking citizenship claims," not simply to obtain financial compensation for the health issues they had incurred but also to benefit from the social welfare they were entitled to.[27] It is a similar "biological citizenship" that is recognized in the case of undocumented migrants who are granted residence permits in France due to a serious disease, and of AIDS patients who become activists of their own medical cause in South Africa.

Both Walter Benjamin and Hannah Arendt had identified this reduction of life to its physical expression and had voiced their concern. In "Critique of Violence," Benjamin states that "the proposition that existence stands higher than a just existence is false and ignominious, if existence is to mean nothing other than mere life," while in her essay *On Revolution*, Arendt denounces "the politically most pernicious doctrine of the modern age, namely that life is the highest good, and that the life process of society is the very center of human endeavor."[28] Unlike these authors, however, my point is not normative but analytical. It is not to condemn the prominence of "life itself," as Benjamin and Arendt name it, over the social and political dimensions that differentiate human beings from other living beings. It is instead to establish its empirical reality and theoretical implications – a move that is all the more important since the fact itself is eclipsed by its naturalization. Indeed,

not only has the physical and biological life a self-evident
material presence, which the social and political life lacks,
but its endangerment arouses compassion and protest, for
instance when pictures of refugees drowned while trying
to reach Europe or of babies affected by a deadly disease
in Africa are displayed in the media, while the threats on
asylum protection generated by the numerous obstacles
opposed to claimants or the risks of unequal access to
treatment resulting from a failing health system do not
provoke such reactions, and are rarely even brought to the
public's attention. A critical approach consists precisely
in giving evidence to the processes through which certain
facts are rendered visible and others invisible, and for the
ethics of life in particular, through which biolegitimacy is
rendered undisputable whereas legal protection and social
justice are more and more easily called into question.

Where does this biolegitimacy stem from? The "doctrine
of the sanctity of life," according to Benjamin, and the idea
that "life is the highest good," according to Arendt, are
for both a survival of the Christian tradition that manifests
itself beyond its apparent decline: "the last mistaken
attempt of the weakened Western tradition to seek the
saint it has lost in cosmological impenetrability," writes
Benjamin; "the modern reversal operated within the fabric
of a Christian society whose fundamental belief in the
sacredness of life has survived, and has even remained
completely unshaken by the secularization and the general
decline of the Christian faith," asserts Arendt.[29] In the
same way as one speaks of a political theology to account
for the permanence of religious concepts in contemporary
politics, one should conceive of an ethical theology to
analyze the persistence of religious concepts in contemporary ethics, however secular the presentation of such an
ethics may be.[30] At the core of this ethical theology is the
valuation of life as the supreme good, epitomized by the
sacrifice of Christ dying on the cross for the salvation of
humankind. Significantly, it is in reference to this Christian
symbolism that 34 prisoners incarcerated in the largest

Ecuadorian correctional facility decided in 2003 to nail themselves to wooden crosses in order to protest against their unlawful detention, as they had not been sentenced and had no prospect of trial, and against the terrible circumstances they were enduring in their jail.[31] By dramatically re-enacting this foundational episode of Christianity and by publicizing it in the media, they opposed their ethical theology of sacrifice to the state's politics of repression. This struggle involved a soteriological aspect since their action was expected to ensure the salvation of future prisoners who would be spared a similar fate. They had indeed announced that they were committed to continue their protest, not until their personal situation was solved, but until legal changes occurred.

Saving others' lives and sacrificing one's own: those are the two symmetrical figures of the ethics of life. It is these figures which are at the heart of the contemporary predicament of humanitarianism and martyrdom in the Occupied Territories of Palestine.

The recent development of humanitarianism is indeed particularly significant evidence of the progress of biolegitimacy.[32] While it is usually assumed that humanitarianism emerged during the earlier movement to end slavery and the slave trade in Britain, France, and the United States, the emergence of humanitarian organizations at the end of the nineteenth century, with the birth of the International Committee of the Red Cross, and its revival a hundred years later with the creation of Doctors Without Borders, mark a major change in the history of humanitarianism: from the battle of Solferino to the Biafra war, the new creed is the saving of lives, initially those of military, and later those of civilians. The main distinctive feature between abolitionist humanitarianism and battlefield humanitarianism – and, by extension, its avatars in response to disaster, famine, or epidemic – is the shift of focus from human rights to saving lives, that is, from life in its social and political dimension, that of the slaves to be freed, to the physical and biological dimension of life, that of the victims to be rescued. In the words of a former president of Doctors Without Borders: "Humanitarian action can still oppose the elimination of part of humanity by exemplifying an art of living founded on the pleasure of unconditionally offering people at risk of death the assistance that will allow them to survive."[33] A prominent figure of moral philosophy in the United States proposed the following syllogism: "Suffering and death from lack of food, shelter and medical care are bad ... By donating to aid agencies, you can prevent suffering and death from lack of food, shelter and medical care, without sacrificing anything nearly as important ... Therefore, if you do not donate to aid agencies, you are doing something wrong."[34] These are definitely extreme forms of reduction of humanitarianism to the mere act of saving lives – and alleviating suffering. Less restrictive, some in the humanitarian movement include other dimensions in their objectives, particularly in terms of human rights, as Doctors of the World's motto exemplifies: "We treat all diseases, even injustice." But the primary *raison d'être* of these organizations remains the existence of endangered lives in contexts of war, disaster, famine, or epidemic – lives to be saved.

Humanitarianism therefore proceeds from an affirmation of the prominence of the physical and biological life of those who are affected by these afflictions. This affirmation is not the sole prerogative of private actors: governments and international aid agencies have adopted it as well. Thus, humanitarianism now forms part of a "global governance" as Mark Duffield designates it.[35] In the contemporary world, there is probably no higher justification for taking action in international relations than that of saving lives. It is the bedrock of the "responsibility to protect" principle, which was voted in 2005 by the United Nations to prevent risks of genocide, war crimes, crimes against humanity, and ethnic cleansing, and which was officially used for the first time in 2011 by France and Britain to launch a military intervention in Libya. Although such an intervention is supposed to occur as a last resort when all diplomatic negotiations and economic sanctions have failed, the new international norm indicates how far states are ready to go against another state's sovereignty in the name of the necessity and the emergency of saving lives, even if in the Libyan case it later appeared that the alleged risk of massacres had been fabricated.

However, the humanitarian imperative is not always confined to situations where its action can be measured in terms of lives saved. The Palestinian Territories are a good example: there are far fewer lives to be saved, in this context, both because the Israeli occupation and the oppression of the Palestinians result in relatively few casualties, except during the bloody but brief Israeli military operations, and because the wounded and diseased can generally be treated in local medical facilities which benefit from international financial support. In this context, the main goal of humanitarian action seems precluded. Yet, besides the UNRWA, the United Nations agency in charge of the more than 5 million Palestinian refugees living in the Occupied Territories and the neighboring countries, several major non-governmental organizations, including Doctors Without Borders and Doctors of the World, have over the past few decades increased their presence in Palestine. But if not to save lives, then to what end? One important humanitarian development, particularly in the Palestinian Territories, concerns mental healthcare. More specifically, trauma and its clinical expression known as post-traumatic stress disorder, which was introduced in the international nosography in 1980, provide reasons for a new potential supply of humanitarian aid which perfectly matches these organizations' interventions.

Representing the potential consequences of experiencing violent events, the common notion of trauma and the psychiatric category of post-traumatic stress disorder are mobilized for both medical assistance, through the care provided to the affected persons, and public testimony, through the language they offer to convey the ordeal of the conflict. Trauma is the moral signified of violence and post-traumatic stress disorder its clinical signifier. Thus, psychic life becomes a substitute for both social life (oppression) and physical life (suffering). However, empirical inquiry shows the limits of the care provided and of the language used.[36] On the one hand, mental health specialists lack the capacity to treat their patients effectively due to the precarious conditions of their intervention, which do not permit the follow-up a regular therapy would offer. On the other hand, they are not in a position to affirm a causal link between the symptoms they identify and the oppression they want to denounce because trauma has complex origins, often related to intimate experiences in childhood.

Under these circumstances, how can the presence of humanitarian workers in the Occupied Territories be justified, beyond the solidarity it manifests? In the absence of lives to be saved, of possibility to properly treat patients, and of evidence of the connection between clinical observations and endured violence, it is through the collection of tragic narratives and the description of disheartening scenes that Doctors Without Borders and Doctors of the World, each in their own way, endeavor to render the experience of occupation, the forms of oppression that characterize it, and the rights violations to which it leads.[37] But these documents pose two sorts of problems, at the interface of ethics and politics. First, the focus on individual stories tends to erase the historical background in which they are inserted, while the phenomenological approach and the clinical interpretation elude the structural conditions that account for them. This blurring of the historical and structural dimensions is particularly evident when the diagnosis of trauma is extended from Palestinians to Israelis who have witnessed attacks either in real life or through television images, since it establishes a moral equivalence between the suffering of the oppressor and that of the oppressed without the differences between their historical and structural dimensions being analyzed.

The mutual recognition of conflict-induced trauma is achieved at the cost of the denial of the irreducibility of respective positions: thus, violence is negated at the very moment it is acknowledged. Second, the representation of Palestinian protagonists, especially young men, as victims undermines their efforts to present themselves as actors of a struggle against the occupier and for an independent state. The trauma certainly renders them more human in the eyes of an international public prompted to perceive them as terrorists, but significantly alters the meaning of their acts of revolt against their oppressor. The psychological language of resilience replaces the political language of resistance. Thus, at the very moment humanitarian organizations endeavor to attest, for an international audience, to the tragedy lived by the Palestinians, they deprive them of a voice as they speak on their behalf using different wording.

Finally, with this dual suspension of the historical and structural dimension on the one hand, and of the protagonists' gesture and voice on the other hand, the very project of ethics of life that could transcend the mere physical fact of being alive, and account for the psychological and social dimension, is confronted with its own contradictions, as it precisely holds its legitimacy only from humanitarian actors' claimed medical expertise. In these conditions, it is not surprising that, as is the case for the discourse on human rights, humanitarian action would often generate mistrust and cynicism in the Territories.[38] Here, such action is faced with its limits far more than it would be on traditional sites of intervention.

But there is a much more troubling challenge for the ethics of life, and it comes from another sort of witnessing: that of martyrs. The ancient Greek term *martus* means witness, and was applied in the New Testament to the Christians who suffered persecution and torture to bear witness to their faith. The Arab word *shahid* has a similar meaning, and is used alike in the Quran to refer to Muslims who accept pain and death to demonstrate their religious beliefs. In both cases, the sacrifice of the earthly life is rewarded by the felicity granted in the afterlife. In Palestine, a martyr is thus any person who dies either actively resisting the occupant or passively enduring the consequences of occupation. But the ethical challenge concerns exclusively the first situation, notably that of suicide attacks against Israelis. These attacks have been almost unanimously condemned, not only by Israel and its allies but also by the Palestinian Authority itself. They have been presented as justifying reprisals against the Palestinian population, including military operations resulting in numerous casualties, and this justification has generally been accepted by most Western countries as a legitimate retaliation whatever its human cost. It would be tempting to interpret the consensus about these armed interventions not only in terms of reaction to the violation of the Israeli sovereignty when the attacks occur on Israeli soil, but also in relation to the moral scandal caused by the deaths of Israeli civilians, who are often described as innocent victims. However, the precedence of the violation of the Palestinian sovereignty, on the one hand, and the disproportionate toll among Palestinian civilians, on the other hand, both provoking no such indignation, at least in the Western world, suggest an additional and more ambiguous explanation.

The Israeli documentary titled *Precious Life* indirectly provides elements of interpretation.[39] It tells the story of a little boy from Gaza born with a deadly autoimmune disease that has already caused the deaths of two of his siblings and for which the only cure is a bone marrow transplant. A compassionate Israeli pediatrician proposes to carry out the procedure in a Tel Aviv hospital and asks a journalist friend to help raise the large sum needed to fund it through a televised plea for help. An anonymous Jewish donor, moved by the child's plight, makes a gift that will allow the operation to take place, provided that a match can be found for the graft. At some point, during the long anxious wait, the reporter engages in conversation

with the mother. Provocatively, he evokes the Palestinian
martyrs ready to die for Jerusalem and declares: "The
whole concept of *shahid* is silly." The young woman
calmly replies that death is normal for her people: "From
the smallest infant to the oldest person, we'd all sacrifice
ourselves for Jerusalem." Shocked, the journalist goes on
asking whether she would let the son whom they are trying
to save from a foretold death become himself a martyr. She
confirms that she would: "Our people get killed dozens at a
time. When one of yours dies, it shakes your entire world.
For us, it's normal. We celebrate when someone becomes
a *shahid*." In voice-over, the reporter manifests his bitterness and discouragement for the young woman's lack of
gratitude and sincerity as he realizes that he is struggling
to save a life which she is actually prepared to let be sacrificed. In fact, the spectator learns a little later that the
young woman made this statement, knowing it was filmed,
in order to silence Palestinians who had expressed suspicion regarding her loyalty after she had publicly praised
the benevolence of the physician and the donor. "I wanted
to prove to the Arabs that I'm still a good Arab – that I'm
still one of them," she says. The film goes on, showing
that shortly before the scheduled bone marrow transplant,
at the end of 2008, the Israeli army launches Operation
Cast Lead, which causes the death of 1,400 Palestinians,
mostly civilians, 400 of them women and children. The
imposed blockade of the Gaza Strip in the aftermath of
the war delays the surgical intervention while the child's
condition rapidly worsens. He is eventually saved just in
time. This happy end is, however, toned down by a parallel
tragedy. During the military operation in Gaza, a grieved
Palestinian surgeon renowned for his peace efforts had
vehemently interpellated the Israeli director: "How long
have you been working on your film? Only to save one life.
But in one second, you ruin people's lives, not just for one
person, but for as many as you can." Three of his daugh-
ters had perished a few minutes before in the bombing
of his house.

In the documentary, and singularly in the two dialogues between the journalist and the woman – the first one, when she claims she would let her son become a martyr, and the second one, when she confesses she was actually responding to her compatriots' mistrust – life is inscribed in two configurations with opposite meanings: one is regarded as humanitarianism, the other as terrorism. In the former, life may be saved. In the latter, life can be sacrificed. Although they belong to the same human being, namely the little boy, these lives are distinct. The life that the pediatrician, with the assistance of the journalist and the donor, is willing to save via a surgical intervention is the physical life. The life that the mother is signifying through the reference to the sacrifice for her people's cause is a political life. However, the film subtly suggests that the two could be bridged: the graft, which is the living matter removed from one person's body and transplanted into someone else's, can be interpreted as a metaphor of the history of the region. Indeed, the explanation given by the pediatrician to the mother, as he informs her about the vital risk incurred by her child, is revealing: "After the transplant, the graft usually reacts adversely to the patient, and at the same time, the body also tries to reject the graft. There is a struggle between two components, which must live side by side, each with its own desires and aspirations. But only if they coexist will they survive." The imagined mapping of the Zionist project and the Palestinian resistance on the little boy's body could not be more explicitly exposed, even opening the possibility of a felicitous conclusion on which both components – biological and political – depend to survive.

Yet the profound disillusion expressed by the journalist after the mother tells him that the fate of her son could be to die as a *shahid* reflects the quandary with which he is confronted and the incomprehension that results from it. "To us, life is precious," he says. "No, life isn't precious," she replies. Two ethics of life are manifested here: for him, life as ends, which must be defended at all cost; for her, life as means, through which freedom can be recovered. Of course, both face their own contradictions: the journalist, when the documentary shows the Israeli army bombing Palestinian houses and killing hundreds of civilians; the young woman, as she admits that she is only addressing her fellows Arabs, as a sign of loyalty. But the disconnection between the two ethics of life fundamentally resides in the very possibility of committing suicide for one's cause. This is where the moral scandal stems from.

In his inquiry into suicide bombing, Talal Asad reflects upon the reasons why this act would cause such horror when the killing by military operations of a host of civilians in the same conflict would not.[40] Beyond the unpredictable and tragic character of this violence, its dramatic bloodbath and the litany of its victims' names, it is the fact that the perpetrator takes his own life to kill others that is incomprehensible and unbearable: he does not leave a bomb behind but uses his own body to cause the massacre. More than a concern for efficacy, the gesture signals a will to signify. The sacrifice is an affirmation of sovereignty. "In the matter of his/her life, the individual has no sovereignty. Suicide is a unique act of freedom, a right that neither the religious authorities nor the nation-state allows," Asad writes. Thus, the person who commits suicide opposes his or her sovereignty to that of the power, be it divine or political.

The evidence of it resides in the fact that this intolerability even concerns individuals who take their own life without causing other deaths. This is why the political gesture of hunger strikers in prison is regarded as scandalous, from Bobby Sands and his fellow inmates, who were left to die in Northern Ireland in 1981, to Marwan Barghouti and the Palestinian security prisoners in Israel, with whom a negotiation was finally conducted in 2017. In Guantanamo the military went as far as to strap detainees to a chair and feed them by force with a stomach tube to prevent their death. Having studied in the early 2000s the hunger strikes of hundreds of Turkish prisoners, mostly

Kurds, to protest against their conditions of confinement, Banu Bargu describes this extreme form of resistance to the authoritarian state, which ended with the death of many of them, as transforming life into a weapon.[41] The silent suicide in the anonymous depth of the carceral institution is the ultimate act through which these men affirmed what she calls "biosovereignty," the sovereignty of life they are ready to sacrifice for their cause. "We have nothing to lose but our bodies. But we have a great world to win!" proclaimed the pamphlet of the Kurds' political movement, paraphrasing the famous words of *The Manifesto of the Communist Party*. Such challenge is unbearable for the state, to the point that, in the United States, even prisoners with a death sentence are subjected to special surveillance and extraordinary precautions to make sure they would not take their own life. They must live so as to be executed. Their suicide would be a formidable failure for the authorities, thus deprived of the sovereign act of killing.

Taking one's physical life to transcend it into a political death, for the Christian martyr in times past or the Muslim *shahid* nowadays, for the Irish prisoner yesterday or the Palestinian detainee today, tests the boundaries of morality.[42] Such gesture affirms an ethics that has become entirely foreign to contemporary Western societies, to such an extent that it cannot even be recognized any more for what it is. In this regard, the random attacks perpetrated since 2015 by Palestinians, some of them adolescents or women, against Israelis, with derisory instruments such as scissors or kitchen knives, signal a remarkable change from previous scenarios of bombing, which supposed technological support and anticipated numerous victims. Hopelessness leads these assailants, operating alone with makeshift weapons, to an act that amounts to a mere suicide. The intolerability of their desperate gesture echoes the intolerability of their endless humiliation. Confronted with the permanent debasement of their lives, these aggressors find in death a way to regain some of their lost value.

Whereas the question of ethical life has been at the heart of moral philosophy since its inception and has recently nourished a fertile field of research in moral anthropology, I have tried to displace it by asking not what is a good life, but rather under which conditions is life itself considered to be a good as such, and even the supreme good. In order to do so, I have drawn two parallels mostly based on empirical research I have conducted over the past two decades. The parallel between immigration and asylum policies in France and public health and social justice debates in South Africa has led me to identify two dimensions of life, biological and political, and to observe that the former tended to prevail over the latter. However, this distinction and this trend were more marked in discourses than in practices, as social agents often tried to resort to both dimensions, but it was definitely easier to mobilize moral sentiments to defend lives threatened by a deadly disease than to protect lives afflicted by violence or inequality. Second, the parallel between the humanitarian gesture of saving the lives of others and the militant act of sacrificing one's life studied in the context of the Israeli occupation of Palestinian Territories has allowed a further exploration of the two dimensions of life through the difference between the fact of keeping alive and the fact of dying for a cause, the latter having become almost incomprehensible while the former receives quasi consensual praise. Beyond this radical opposition, it is, however, possible to recognize a similar premise: life itself is the highest good possessed by human beings, which explains why it being rescued in one case and sacrificed in the other is subject to such a crucial ethical investment. Thus, there is not one but several ethics of life, some being dominant, while others are rejected or repressed.

Although I have wanted not to elude delicate topics – the sacredness of life and the meaning of its sacrifice, which both generate passions – I have strived to avoid judgmental statements and normative stances. The point is not to decide whether it is a good thing that life might

be deemed the supreme good, or a bad thing to not understand any more that one might want to sacrifice it for a
cause, but to analyze the contemporary transformations
through which life is apprehended. What is gained and
what is lost, what is made visible and what is rendered
unspeakable in this ethical shift toward biolegitimacy:
these are the issues I have addressed. And my conclusions
are that biological citizenship tends to affect the significance of social rights, that the rise in the recognition of
physical life is frequently accompanied by a decline in the
import of political life, that the legitimacy of humanitarian
emergency diminishes the power of the call for social
justice, and that the self-evident justification of saving lives
renders unthinkable the meaning of sacrificing one's life
for a cause. These affirmations are of course too general,
and would certainly need to be tempered, adjusted, or
refined to account for the complexity of empirical situations, as I have done in previous works. But they emphasize the stakes of what has become the almost uncontested
salience of biolegitimacy in contemporary societies, starting with Mahmoud Darwish's interrogation in the epigraph: is life defined only as the opposite of death still life?
These stakes connect the ethics of life with both the forms
of life, in the tension between the natural and the social,
and the politics of life, through the exploration of the way
in which human beings are evaluated and governed.

Yet one troubling question remains. The characteriza-
tion of life as supreme good, the distinction between physical life and social life, and the analysis of the privilege that
contemporary societies tend to grant to the former at the
detriment of the latter, as I have described, seem in fact
underpinned by an implicit hierarchy that can be misleading and even dangerous. Indeed, if one adopts the Aristotelian definition of man as *zoon politikon*, there is little
doubt that what separates human beings from other living
species, namely their political life, is superior to what they
have in common with them, namely their biological life.
The "simple fact of being alive" for Benjamin, "life itself"

for Arendt, and "bare life" for Agamben, are obviously, from their perspective, lower forms of life, to which human beings should not be debased. They oppose to it "just existence," "the idea of freedom," and "qualified life," respectively, all concepts that elevate human beings above other living beings. This terminology and the conceptualization that underlies it were meant to account for the way human lives were treated by the authorities or society, and not, as they have often been mistakenly interpreted, to account for the way human beings actually live. That the attitude of many states toward refugees seems to reduce their existence to its most basic expression does not imply that these refugees let themselves be reduced to it. The regrettable confusion between the two interpretations tends to devalue the life of refugees, a situation, however, which they tenaciously oppose, resisting the erosion of their dignity. The same applies to all individuals confronted by the extreme hardships of a precarious life.

It is while doing fieldwork in South African townships and former homelands with people living with AIDS that I became aware of the necessity to acknowledge the difference between the way lives are treated and the way they are lived, and of the importance of rehabilitating the mere fact of being alive as a necessary condition for the self-realization of a form of life.[43] The majority faced the ordeal of extreme poverty and suffered from severe complications of the disease. As the advanced stage of their affliction had made them aware of the little time that they had left to live, many of them were reinventing their life in multiple ways, striving to become a moral person after having had a troubled existence, or turning to activism for universal access to antiretroviral drugs to help other patients. The life in which they fully invested was both biological (they developed a special, intimate, even personified relationship with their disease, their body, their medicines, their lymphocytes) and social (often with a strong religious component but also sometimes a political dimension). What they aspired to, they often said, was "normal life." One of them explained: "Normal life is what people live out of it: having food in your stomach, having somebody next to you, being respected in your community." Such a modest but sensible ethic of life did not separate the physical, the affective, and the moral.

These conversations struck me all the more since in the same period I happened to read the last interview that Jacques Derrida had given before his death, when he knew his days were numbered.[44] "Since certain health problems have become so urgent," he said, "the question of survival or of reprieve, a question that has always haunted me, literally every instant of my life, in a concrete and unrelenting fashion, has come to have a different resonance." In this tragic moment, survival – in the dual meaning of "continuing to live" and "surviving death," *fortleben* and *überleben*, in other words, being still present in the world for some time and remaining present to it via the works left behind – combined the physical life that was fading away and the social life that prolonged it, rehabilitating the former to the rank of the latter.

In his memoir about the time he spent in the Buchen-wald concentration camp, Robert Antelme evokes what survival practices meant in the Gandersheim commando to which he belonged in the following way:[45] "The experiences of the one who feeds on peelings is one of the ultimate situations of resistance. It is also nothing other than the extreme experience of the proletarian's condition." It associates, on one side, "the disdain of the one who has forced him into this state, and who does everything to keep him there, so that this state apparently accounts for the whole person of the oppressed and thereby justifies his oppressor," and, on the other side, "the claim, in the relentless effort to eat to stay alive, of the highest of values." Thus, "struggling to live, he struggles to provide justifications to all values, including those which his oppressor, while falsifying them, tries to reserve for his own exclusive enjoyment." Defending one's right to stay alive under these circumstances partakes of a superior ethical commitment even if it is difficult to comprehend "the greatness that may be found in this act." For Antelme, the materiality of physical life that must be preserved in this debasement of the human condition is inseparable from political life – which is underlined by the reference to the proletarian and the language of oppression. Hence, this glimmer of hope amid the darkness: "The prospects for the liberation of all mankind pass through this 'fallen condition'." Indeed, the risk of dehumanization does not reside in these attempts to debase, "which in no way affect the integrity" of those who are subjected to them, but in the "weaknesses with infinitely more import," such as not having shared a meager meal, as one should, with one's companion in misfortune: "The error of conscience is not to fall down but to lose sight of the fact that the downfall must be of everyone and for everyone." This is probably where the ethics of life meets the ethical life.

III
Politics of Life

Although our life is often worthless, yet it is life and not simply extracting square roots.

Dostoevsky, *Notes from the Underground*, 1992 [1864]

That society has a collective responsibility in the good government of human beings and that consequently it must be organized in order to ensure a good life for all has been a major theme in philosophy since Plato's *Republic* and Aristotle's *Politics*. In the contemporary world, determining the right balance with respect to the intervention of the state into the life of its citizens in order to ensure both equality and liberty is still an object of intense debates among political theorists as well as politicians, whether it concerns economic regulation or social welfare, public security or internet monitoring. The stakes at play in these issues are evidently ethical as much as political, especially when it comes to precarious forms of life, those of individuals or groups particularly vulnerable to ethical breaches for whom political action can prove to be crucial.

To reflect upon the good government of human lives, philosophers often tend to refer to classical theories, implicitly considering that there is a sort of continuity in problems and solutions since Antiquity, as if the concepts of justice, equality, liberty, and democracy offered a suitable language to analyze politics trans-historically. But is there such a continuity? Not according to Michel Foucault. For him, an important rupture took place during the eighteenth century, when power and knowledge started to invest human life entirely, from birth to death, through sexuality and reproduction, via healthcare and pension systems, in sum, everything that has to do with the human species and its environment. This is what he terms "biopower," and more specifically "biopolitics," a concept that has given rise to a considerable literature in the social sciences. The point I want to argue is that biopolitics does not correspond to what its etymology suggests. It deals less with politics than governmentality and has more to do with population than life: biopolitics is not a politics of life but a government of populations. Moreover, it emphasizes technologies of action at the expense of its content: biopolitics concerns the way in which power operates, particularly through the conduct of conducts, and not what politics does with human lives and how it treats them. It is this other dimension of the relations between politics and life that I am interested in, and to distinguish it, I will speak of politics of life. The moment one adopts this perspective – asking not how technologies govern populations but what politics does to human lives – the question of inequality becomes essential, since not all lives are treated equally and since these differences in treatment convey differences in the value they are granted. But this inequality contradicts the foundation of the ethics of life, which is based on the sacredness of life: being a supreme and inalienable good, its value is consequently supposed equal for all human beings. It is this fundamental tension between ethics of life and politics of life that I propose to analyze here, first by showing, via a genealogical approach, how the value of lives came to be quantified, and, therefore, became the object of disparities, and second, by examining – through ethnographic as well as statistical illustrations from the research I conducted in France, South Africa, and the United States – how social disparities reveal moral hierarchies in the valuation of human lives.

Few of Foucault's concepts have received as much attention as biopolitics. Yet its appearance in his works is fugacious, its definition barely outlined, and its development several times announced but never achieved. Indeed, at the end of *The Will to Knowledge*, Foucault succinctly analyzes the shift from sovereignty to biopower and the emergence of life as the foundational stake of Western politics, which he describes as the "threshold of modernity." He distinguishes two dimensions in this process: the "anatomopolitics of the human body," which consists of the "disciplines" exercised on the physical "machine" to optimize its capabilities, extort its forces, and increase its usefulness and docility, in order to integrate it into the social and economic system; and the "biopolitics of the population," which entails the "regulation" of the human "species" through the administration of birth, death, health, housing, and migrations.[1] That such biopolitics – and also anatomopolitics, for that matter – appeared, as Foucault argues, in eighteenth-century Western societies is certainly disputable since complex systems of rules, institutions, and practices dedicated to the governing of populations, including birth control, family organization, collective hygiene, and so on, already existed in the first-century Roman Empire as well as the fifteenth-century Inca Empire, among others.[2] But the most intriguing element in the history of this concept is that its very inventor never engaged it fully, even in his lectures at the Collège de France.

In 1976, in *Society Must Be Defended*, he evokes it in two pages, proposing a mere enumeration of its domains, which correspond mostly to demography, epidemiology, and public health. A definition follows: "Biopolitics deals with the population ... as a problem that is at once scientific and political." At the beginning of *Security,*

Territory, Population, in 1978, he announces that he wants to start "studying something that I have called ... biopower," that is, "the set of mechanisms through which the basic biological features of the human species became the object of a political strategy." But the lectures actually focus on governmentality, security systems, and *raison d'état*, the word "biopolitics" being mentioned only once in passing. Even more significantly, the following year, in *The Birth of Biopolitics*, his intention, well indicated in the title, is not pursued any further. Having explained in the opening pages that "the analysis of biopolitics can only get under way when we have understood the general regime of this governmental reason," that is, "liberalism," Foucault has to admit, in the summary published at the end of the year, that the "course ended up being devoted entirely to what should have been only its introduction."[3] From then on, he mostly employs himself to ethical questions. He never returns to biopolitics.

So, what are we left with in order to analyze this concept? I am limiting my discussion here to Foucault's thesis but it should not be forgotten that, as shown by Thomas Lemke, there is both a forgotten genealogy to be traced at least to the German *Lebensphilosophie* and the Swedish political theorist Rudolf Kjellén, who appears to be the first to introduce the term "biopolitics" at the beginning of the twentieth century, and a rich cartography of contemporary approaches, including the works of Michael Hardt and Toni Negri on "biopolitical production."[4] To focus on Foucault's formulation, by far the most innovative and influential, it can be said that the idea of biopolitics proceeds from a fertile intuition but is also a source of confusion: a fertile intuition according to which societies have increasingly developed mechanisms to regulate the existence of human beings; a source of confusion, as its etymology can be misleading if one considers what it effectively means. "What, precisely, are 'politics' and 'life' for Foucault?" wonders Roberto Esposito. He points out that, in the same way as one might have reproached the

author of *The History of Sexuality* for the lack of clarifica-
tion around his conception of politics, one could criticize
him for the way "life remains little problematized" in his
work.[5] But we can even go further and assert that biopolitics might be a matter of neither politics nor life. Indeed,
as regards the prefix "bio," not only does the notion of
life alternatively and indiscriminately refer to the biological process, the social body, and the human species, but
above all, this biopolitics does not even concern life as
such, but instead population: it is actually a demopoli-
tics. Similar reservations can be expressed with respect to
the root "politics," since it broadly pertains to modalities
of regulation, rationales of control, and ways of governing, rather than the content of biopolitics, its debates and
action, and its stakes and conflicts: therefore, it would be
more accurate to speak about biogovernmentality.

In fact, the omission of life and the elision of politics are
linked. One could be inclined to interpret this dual absence
as Foucault's reluctance to incorporate social criticism in
his genealogical critique. It is the emergence of new "prob-
lematizations" that he wants to uncover, and not what
underpins them or results from them. He is interested in
the way in which what seems today self-evident emerged
– birth control, measurement of mortality, management of
public hygiene, control of migration flows – rather than
in the social forces at play in this process. An amendment
should however be added to this general observation, since
in the few pages he dedicates to biopower in *The Will to
Knowledge*, he writes that the latter "was without question an indispensable element in the development of capitalism," which "would not have been possible without the
controlled insertion of bodies into the machinery of production and the adjustment of the phenomena of population to economic processes."[6] Nevertheless, this is virtually
his only concession to Marxism or, more generally, social
criticism in his writings on biopolitics. In his later lectures, liberalism substitutes for capitalism; in other words,
market mechanisms replace relations of production, and

social determinism, which was notably present in his study of illegalisms, fades away. What politics does to life – or lives – is not what interests him, nor is it the differential way in which it does so. The word "inequality" does not belong to his vocabulary.

This eclipse of life and the evanescence of politics have for that matter not remained unnoticed by the theorists who, after Foucault, made the concept of biopolitics their own. Discussions regarding this dual paradox deployed in two symmetrical perspectives: one pertains to social criticism and questions the biologization of politics; the other belongs to the genealogical tradition and questions the politicization of biology.[7] For Ferenc Fehér and Agnes Heller, politics has virtually disappeared from biopolitics, which is less a critique of Foucault than of contemporary societies. More precisely, according to these authors, biopolitics is antithetic to traditional politics. While the latter was universalist and put freedom and liberation from tyranny above other values, the former is particularist and promotes social identities relying on supposedly natural grounds, whether sexual or racial, related to health or environment. Biopolitics is a politics of difference that justifies itself in the language of biology. It is about singularity rather than plurality. For Agamben, conversely, life is missing from biopolitics, and it is for him conspicuous that Foucault would not have seen that totalitarian regimes represented the most extreme expression of the latter with the separation they instituted between the natural and the political. More specifically, in his view, the concentration camp is the culmination of biopolitics, inasmuch as it reduces prisoners to the sole quest of their physical survival. Thus, he reveals the fundamental truth of the sovereign power, which stems from the politicization of bare life. Regardless of the differences in their analysis, it is significant that both the Hungarian theorists and the Italian philosopher acknowledge their intellectual debt to Hannah Arendt.[8] Indeed, the author of *The Human Condition* distinguishes labor, the biological driving force of

the principle of subsistence, from work and action, which
correspond to the making of the world and to the relationships between human beings, respectively, and thus as a
last resort to politics. But, Arendt regretfully observes,
what characterizes modernity is the rising import of the
biological and the gradual decline of the political.

It is from this perspective that one could analyze the
renewed interest for biopolitics within the social sciences,
particularly in the studies on life sciences and their implications in numerous domains of human life. The deciphering
of the human genome and the scientific breakthroughs it
produced – from the creation of genetic banks supposed
to transform our understanding of the anthropology of
populations to the development of genetic tests assumed
to reduce the incidence of certain diseases and enhance
the efficacy of certain drugs – generated reflections on
what these advances in knowledge and technology could
lead to, some worrying about the biologization of the
world, the demiurgic power on the living, and a possible eugenic shift, others considering more favorably the
potential benefits of biomedicine for public health and of
bioeconomics for capitalism.[9] However, the understand-
able fascination that these scientific achievements, technological innovations, and intellectual challenges exert on
social scientists tends to redouble the celebration of these
forms of biopolitics. Even the concerns expressed about
their potential consequences amount to taking the scientific discourse at face value and consolidating its perfor-
mative function. The – exciting or frightening – image of
this futuristic project thus contributes to the exaltation
of the relations between politics and life. Moreover, it
relies on the implicit representation of an undifferentiated
domain in which the contemporary transformations of the
relations between politics and life would affect everyone
in a similar fashion, independently of their social category and geographical inscription, whether upper classes
or ethnoracial minorities, citizens of wealthy nations as
much as inhabitants of poor countries. Thus understood,

biopolitics risks focusing on the exceptional rather than the ordinary, eluding the major disparities existing in its implementation. This is why my critical take on biopolitics is not about what biopolitics represents but what it does not – or, more accurately, what the representation of the world it provides does not permit to represent. In talking about politics of life rather than biopolitics, I thus propose to restore the relation between politics and life, that is, on the one hand, to take seriously the fact that it is literally a matter of politics rather than governmentality and of human life rather than population, and, on the other hand, to consider this relation from the angle of the way politics treats human lives so as to reintroduce the ordinary and the social. To illustrate the difference of perspective I attempt to draw between biopolitics and politics of life, we can take the case of humanitarian actions. An approach in terms of biopolitics will be interested in the technologies deployed, the analysis of problems and solutions in terms of population, the resort to demography and epidemiology to identify health priorities, and the establishment of an infrastructure of camps to concentrate people in a more operational way for intervention. By contrast, an approach in terms of politics of life will be looking at how the recognition of life as supreme good justifies the breach in state sovereignty, how tragic choices are made to decide under the constraint of limited resources which patients will be treated and which lives will be saved, and finally how a hierarchy in the worth of lives is implicitly established between national and expatriate personnel by humanitarian organizations in terms of salary, social protection, and rights within the charity, as well as by belligerents who generally kill the former but abduct the latter to request ransoms. In sum, biopolitics is about the framing of the government of human beings, while the politics of life pertain to its substance. One is interested in the techniques and rationales of population management, whereas the others focus on the differentiation in the treatment of lives and its meaning in terms of unequal worth.

Therefore, politics of life are directly related to ethics of life. If the latter, as I have defined them, analyze the absolute value of life and decrypt the stakes of biolegitimacy, the former examine the relative evaluation of lives and critique the inequalities they unveil. It is thus a shift from the singular to the plural – from life in general to lives in particular. It is also a move from the normative to the empirical – from ideal value to actual value.[10] What are lives worth in different contexts or milieus? What do these variations reveal about the corresponding societies? To explore the tension between the valuation of life as supreme good and the formidable disparities in the evaluation of lives in the real world, I will analyze, first, the way in which the monetary appreciation of lives developed over the last 2,000 years, then the way in which differences in the value of lives are translated in the United States, South Africa, and France.

It is in economic language that the valuation of a human life is the most explicitly – some would say, the most crudely – apprehended, since, as Thomas Schelling argues, economics provides the translation of an abstract principle into a measurable fact, which generally represents the financial compensation of a death.[11] Consequently, an examination of the sums allocated in these circumstances and of the reasoning underlying the calculations to determine these sums provides a straightforward method to assess the range of what is probably the most fundamental inequality: that of the worth of lives.

In *The Philosophy of Money*, Georg Simmel proposes a genealogy of the practices used for the evaluation of lives. He bases his analysis on the way in which, in cases of homicide, the murderer's relatives were supposed to compensate the victim's family.[12] "The atonement of murder by payment of money" is "so frequent in primitive societies that it makes specific examples unnecessary," he notes, adding nevertheless that the significance of this practice is not so much its frequency "as the intensity with which the relationship between human value and money value dominates legal conceptions." He provides the illustration of early Anglo-Saxon England, where the killing of a person led to the payment of a wergild, which literally means in Old English, "the valuation of man." The sum was calculated in fractions or multiples of the value of a free man, which was fixed at 200 shillings. Even the assassination of the King had a monetary equivalent, although the amount of the fine was so high that it could not be paid by a single person or even the group to which that person belonged, with the consequence that slavery or even death could be the practical outcome. This practice of repaying a sum to the victim's relatives to redress their loss has not disappeared. For instance, it is still in use in Islamic law.[13] The *diyya*, often translated as "blood money," serves as an alternative to the *qisas*, which corresponds to the implementation of the principle of an eye for an eye: instead of having the murderer executed, the family of the victim can request a financial compensation, the amount of which will be determined by a judge.

But, in numerous societies, the assessment of the value of a person is not only associated with homicides: it is also involved in marriages through the payment of a dowry by the family of the bride or, conversely, of a bride price by the family of the groom. Marriage has been studied for a long time by anthropologists, in terms of rules of alliance, and by economists, in terms of matrimonial markets.[14] In this dual perspective, the payment, in kind or in cash to the family of the bride or the groom can be considered as the economic translation of the social exchange that marriage represents, whether it be, for the dowry, to facilitate the wife's moving in with her husband, or for the bride price, to offer a way for the family of the latter to compensate that of the former.

However, when one member of the couple is affected by a specific condition, making it more difficult for him or her to get married, the difference in terms of dowry or bride price becomes indicative of his or her loss of value. Such is the case in Senegal for handicapped individuals, as I have shown via a series of biographies collected in Dakar and its surroundings.[15] If the disabled person is a man, the bride price paid by his family will be increased; if a woman, the amount will be on the contrary diminished. It can even be waived and the bride be "offered in *taako*," which means that the groom will marry her without providing any compensation. It should be noted that this practice also concerns women deemed unfit for marriage for social reasons, for instance widows or divorced women considered too old to give birth and to support themselves. While such financial arrangements often prove beneficial to prevent handicapped persons from remaining socially isolated, the variations in the amount paid by the groom's family reveal a deep gender inequality: whereas disability depreciates the person in both sexes, women are symbolically more affected since the decline of their value, sometimes even reduced to zero, on the marriage market, is more humiliating than for men is the increase in the amount their family has to pay to conclude the alliance.

Thus, whether it is for the repayment of a murder or the payment for a marriage, the economic evaluation of individuals has a social function: to dispense justice and avoid retaliation, in the first case; to link families and integrate physically or even socially disadvantaged individuals, in the second. In its principle, the establishment of a material equivalent for human beings thus facilitates social cohesion. However, based on several historical illustrations, Simmel notes that a major transformation occurred when the economic rationale in which the interest of the group prevailed was replaced by a reasoning built on the monetary estimation of the individual. Here, the reparation for homicides is again instructive. Whereas the victim's parents initially demanded variable amounts to compensate their loss, the legal system progressively changed and resulted, as previously discussed, in specific sums of wergild, which implied that a specific value was attributed to the "man in himself." This stabilization of the wergild in the law signals a shift from a "subjective utilitarian valuation of human life into the objective notion that man has a specific value," giving birth to a differential evaluation in the worth of lives.

Yet, in the Christian world, such politics of life contradicted the ethics of life, which affirmed two connected but distinct principles: the sanctity of life and the absolute value of the human. The combination of the two rendered a monetary valuation of human life theoretically impossible. The latter was incommensurable in the dual sense that it could not be measured and could not be evaluated. In a classical article, the ethnologist Kenneth Read echoes this view as he draws a parallel between Christian morality and the morality of the Gahuku-Gama, a group from the Highlands of Papua New Guinea.[16] "From the standpoint of Christian ethics, men are moral equals," he asserts. "As persons, their value is constant ... This worth is inalienable; it is also intrinsic, belonging to all men irrespective of status or individual accomplishments. The absolute value of the human person is prior to all other created values." Conversely, for the Gahuku-Gama, the value granted to human beings is "dependent on the position they occupy within a system of inter-personal and inter-group relationships." Consequently, when a murder is committed, the social response, which is modulated according to the status of the culprit and the victim, reveals "the moral nature of the social bonds between individuals and groups of individuals rather than the inviolability of human life itself." Thus, for Read, the contrast cannot be greater between Papuan and Christian norms and values. His interpretation is, however, manifestly biased for methodological as much as ideological reasons since, unlike what he did for the Gahuku-Gama, whose moral system and social practices he thoroughly studied, he relies for what regards Christian ethics on the official dogma, as taught by the catechesis, rather than on the way it is actually

carried out. The result is an archetypal reading of the
doctrine, far from the reality of the Christian world.

Indeed, although the claim that human life is inviolable
and consequently that all human beings have equal value
and inalienable dignity is perfectly in line with the Christian principles recently reaffirmed in John Paul II's *Encycli-
cal Evangelium Vitae*, it does not correspond to the
historical evidence.[17] Suffice to read the inquiry conducted
by Reinhart Koselleck on the "asymmetric countercon-
cepts," that is, pairs of terms used to refer to – and oppose
– "them" and "us" in various periods of the history of
Western societies.[18] In the case of the Christians/Heathens
pair in particular, he shows the occurrence of a radical
divide, which did not exist during Antiquity with the Hel-
lenes/Barbarians pair, between those who have faith and
will be saved and those who did not convert and will be
damned. From Paul to Augustine, the canon resorts to a
semantics which clearly delineates two categories of human
beings, with quite different moral values and eschatologi-
cal destinies. In its transposition into the practices of the
Church, this distinction has served to racialize, vilify, and
even kill Muslims in the Crusades, Jews under the Inquisi-
tion, and more broadly "*infideles, impii, increduli, perfidi,
inimici Dei*." Exclusive, the Christian politics of life has
for a long time been far removed from its ethical ideal.

The emergence of the insurance industry in the nineteenth century, as studied by Viviana Zelizer for the United
States, was a decisive moment for the confrontation
between the Christian ideology of sacred life and primacy
of the human, and the economic rationale of monetary
equivalent to life and hierarchy in the worth of human
beings.[19] Indeed, the conception of a system in which individuals paid regular premiums for the accumulated capital
to be given to their relatives after their death conveyed the
idea of financialization of life and the perspective of disparities in the amounts provided to families. "Life insurance was felt to be sacrilegious," Zelizer explains, "because
its ultimate function was to compensate the loss of a father

and a husband with a check to his widow and orphans. Critics objected that this turned man's sacred life into an 'article of merchandise'." The Mennonites went as far as to excommunicate those of their members who insured their life. Confronted with this virulent opposition, insurance companies worked to transform the image of their industry. In order to have this financial innovation accepted by the Church as well as laypeople, a dual process of "ritualization" of life insurance and "sacralization" of money was undertaken: customers were lauded for their "wise and generous provision" and their concern for the well-being of their dependents after their decease; "new notions of immortality" were introduced, through which the money returned to the family was described as honoring the memory of the deceased. This was actually part of a broader endeavor undertaken to moralize the representation of capitalism among the public. In this particular case, it meant proposing a form of transcendence of the financial world via an edifying speech on the "good death" of those who had behaved responsibly during their worldly life so as to leave resources to those who survived them. As one can expect, the material immortality that insurance companies promised to their customers revealed profound disparities.

The idea that human life could have a monetary equivalent, therefore, gradually imposed itself. It is indeed telling to compare the controversies around the creation of life insurance at the beginning of the nineteenth century and the polemics surrounding the financial compensations for lives lost that took place at the end of the twentieth century. Whereas, in the first case, the question was whether one could, legally or morally, give an economic value to human life, in the second one, it had become whether the amount granted to the relatives was sufficient. Thus, in South Africa, after the Truth and Reconciliation Commission had established the official list of the crimes committed under apartheid, the families of the victims of the regime had to wait five years to obtain financial reparations and

the one-time payment they received was less than a quarter
of what the commission had recommended: the initial
impatience of those who had painfully testified turned into
anger as the amount of the indemnity was deemed "insult-
ing."[20] But when contrasting the two periods, one should
acknowledge that the rationale for compensation of lives
lost differs from that of life insurance, not only because it
is retrospective in the first case and prospective in the
second one, but also, and above all, because the latter
proceeds from individual choices while the former stems
from a collective decision.

However justified it may therefore seem today to the
majority, the idea that the harm done to certain individuals
or groups should, both morally and financially, be regarded
as a collective debt that is owed to these individuals and
groups is of recent introduction. It can be seen as a con-
tinuation of the policy of compensation for workers inca-
pacitated by an accident, which had been initiated in
Prussia at the end of the nineteenth century and later dis-
seminated across Europe and North America. But compared to this original model, the current system of
indemnity presents two major differences which result in
a significant widening of the range of reparations. First,
instead of considering that only the individual, group, or
company involved is liable, and therefore required to compensate the victims, it is now society as a whole that is
held accountable for the harm done to some of its members
when the responsible party is not solvent or not identifiable. Thus, special funds and specific institutions have
been created in many countries for the indemnity of various
hazards, from hurricane to burglary, industrial accident to
terrorist attack. Second, the scope of victimhood has been
substantially broadened so as to include people who are
indirectly concerned, such as witnesses, even viewers of
traumatic events. It can even include individuals or groups
several generations after the facts, as is the case for slavery
and slave trade reparation claims, although these should
be understood less as being simply the reminder of a

painful history than as representing the recognition of present injustice, that is, the existence of profound marks left by yesterday's practices in today's situations. Both evolutions reveal major transformations in the relation to adversity. Long ignored or discredited, victims have acquired over the past few decades a legitimate status and a positive image.[21] It is often an entire nation that feels indebted to them.

The recognition of victims, with the corollary obligation to compensate their loss, has given rise to complex systems of quantification of the worth of lives, generating disputes and disparities. In the United States, the creation by the Congress of the September 11 Victim Compensation Fund in the aftermath of 9/11 provides an illustration.[22] The result of a long assessment during which the lawyer Kenneth Feinberg met with the relatives of the victims to best determine the individual consequences of the tragedy, the process was nevertheless criticized, as had been life insurance practices in the nineteenth century and financial compensation of hazards in the twentieth century: some opposed the principle of a monetary equivalence to lives lost, which they deemed literally inestimable; others contested the sums, especially as payment would be done on condition that claimants would not pursue any other legal proceedings in the future. But disparities in the allocated sums were less debated. The calculations were taking into account an estimation of the economic loss resulting from the casualty to which was added a fixed amount for the surviving partner and children, when there were any, in reparation of their suffering. The sum given to the families varied between $788,000 for low-income groups and over $6 million for high-income ones. On average, the compensation for the death of a woman was evaluated at only 63 percent of the amount awarded for the death of a man.

Even more striking than these class and gender disparities, albeit little noticed, are the differences in the treatment of various tragic events. Neither the casualties of the Oklahoma City bombing which killed 168 people and injured 680 in 1995, nor the victims of Hurricane Katrina, which caused 1,245 deaths in 2005, led to financial compensations from the authorities. In fact, rather than the type of tragedy or even the seriousness of the damages, it is the emotion provoked and the moral community imagined that seem to explain these differences. Launched against the economic heart of the country by an external foe that could immediately be personified and demonized, the 9/11 attacks united the nation. Conversely, with the Oklahoma City bombing, the fact that the enemy was a young white middle-class war veteran who had served in Iraq rendered the building of a common affliction more difficult. Likewise, in Louisiana, the victims were mostly poor black people, which limited the possibility of a shared grief in a country where the contrasting reactions to the disaster revealed the scars of its long history of racism and discrimination. In the differential treatment of these events, a combination of often implicit elements thus pertains to the social, political, emotional, and moral evaluation of which lives matter and, when lost, which deserve reparation.

In the end, the tension between an ethics of life, which proclaims that life is sacred and therefore priceless, and a politics of life, which acknowledges the necessity of financial reparation for lives lost and consequently calls for their fair pricing, can only deepen as the valuation of a life implies not only that a monetary equivalent is established, but also that this process leads to unequal indemnity. The compensation of casualties on battlefields is in that regard a striking illustration. For each Iraqi civilian killed mistakenly, or deliberately, by the army of the United States, the financial reparation when the latter admits its responsibility – which is a rare occurrence – is approximately $4,000. For a U.S. soldier killed in action or in an accident, the total benefits paid to the spouse and children can exceed $800,000.[23] The ratio in terms of what life is worth is 1 to 200. Moreover, taking into account the statistics for the first eight years of the conflict, all the families of the 4,500 U.S. military casualties were entitled to financial reparation, whereas very few of the families of the more than 500,000 Iraqis, mostly civilians, who died as a result of the invasion of their country were deemed eligible to such indemnity. Additionally, the counting accuracy to the unit for the victims, in the first case, and the vagueness of their number, rounded to the nearest hundred thousand, in the second case, crudely confirm the difference in the worth granted to their respective lives.

However, the economic valuation is only one of the possible indicators of the inequalities in the worth of lives within a given society or across countries. It measures and reveals them – at least in one of their dimensions. It may even contribute toward consolidating or legitimizing them. But it does not create them. So, what does? An interesting answer to that question was formulated more than a century ago. In an essay on what was then significantly termed "moral statistic," Maurice Halbwachs contested the fact that death would be a sort of fatality, independent of human intervention. He writes: "We forget that death, and the age when it occurs, result above all from life and the circumstances in which it unfolded, these conditions being at least as much social as physical."[24] For him, the main explanation for the variations in mortality observed from one region or one country to another resides in the "importance given to human life" that can be interpreted as a sort of "judgment of society regarding the life" of its members: "There are good reasons to think that a society has the mortality that suits it, and that the number of deaths and their distribution at different ages accurately expresses the importance that a society attaches to prolonging life more or less." Fifty years later, Georges Canguilhem adopts this thesis and comments on it by insisting on the role of public health practices: "The techniques of collective hygiene which tend to prolong human life, or the habits of negligence which result in shortening it, depending on the value attached to life in a given society, are in the end a value judgment expressed in the abstract number which is the average human life span."[25] However, he adds a substantial element, affirming that what he calls "the socially normative life span" would appear more clearly "if, instead of considering the average life span in a national society taken as a whole, we broke this society down into classes, occupations, etc." so as to bring into light the impact of the "levels of life" on this indicator. Thus, for both Halbwachs and Canguilhem, it is "the judgment of society regarding life" and the "value attached to life" which, in the end, account for the differences between countries and between social categories. Here, the valuation is not only economical, but above all, moral. The differential allocation of values also affects the lives of human beings, depending on the place they inhabit or the milieu they belong to, is thus translated in concrete terms in the way society treats them and, finally, in what is – technically and symbolically – their life expectancy.

This idea certainly goes against the commonly held viewpoint, from which death is a natural phenomenon determined by individual biological characteristics and behavioral traits: bad genes and bad habits would explain why some live longer than others. But it also goes against the very foundations of the democratic regimes which have the equality of citizens and the right to life as principles. The Declaration of Independence of the United States, for instance, affirms "that all men are created equal, that they are endowed with certain alienable rights, that among these are life, liberty and the pursuit of happiness"; yet it is noteworthy that the early draft written by Thomas Jefferson contained a substantial passage condemning slavery, which, after intense debates among the delegates gathered in Philadelphia, was deleted in the final version, thus inscribing implicitly the inequality of human beings and the alienability of human life in the act of birth of the nation.[26] Even the author of the famous *Discourse Upon the Origin and the Foundation of the Inequality of Mankind* resists the idea of a link between the moral and the physical dimensions of inequality: "I discern two sorts of inequality in the human species," writes Jean-Jacques Rousseau in the opening pages:[27] "the first I call natural or physical because it is established by nature, and consists in difference in age, health, strength of the body, and the qualities of the mind or soul"; and "the second, we might call moral or political inequality because it derives from a sort of convention, and is established, or at least authorized by the consent of men," and which "consists of the different privileges which some enjoy to the prejudice of others." But there is no point in inquiring "whether there is not some essential connection between the two types of inequality," as it would imply asking "whether those who command are necessarily better than those who obey" and "whether bodily or intellectual strength, wisdom and virtue are always to be found in individuals, in proportion to their power or wealth." Thus, if Rousseau rejects the hypothesis of a possible link between the two sorts of inequality, it is because he only conceives of it as a possible justification for moral inequalities by natural inequalities. He does not imagine the opposite relation, namely that the former could be the source of the latter, which would at least suppose that these inequalities could precisely not be thought of as "natural." It is clear from these various examples that the very idea of a social inequality in human lives confronts the preconceptions of common sense, of political rhetoric, and even of philosophical thinking. As Lorraine Daston asserts, in order to be able to think life in terms of probability, or "life chances," rather than fate, or "the wheel of fortune," two preconditions are necessary:[28] "the notion of statistical regularities, and the belief in the existence of homogeneous categories of people to which the regularities apply." Neither of these ideas is intuitive. It is only at the beginning of the nineteenth century that moral statistics begin to fulfill these preconditions, with the first mortality surveys based on socioeconomic categories or characteristics.[29] Two centuries later, demography and epidemiology have produced an impressive amount of evidence on disparities in life expectancy.

Indeed, statistics are necessary to bring into light these social inequalities, which are often deeply buried in the opacity of bodies. Some deaths are seen as natural, whether they be the consequences of cardiovascular diseases, cancers, diabetes, cirrhosis, or infections. Others are perceived as randomly distributed, such as in cases of car or occupational accidents, homicides or suicides. Yet bivariate and multivariate analyses using mortality or morbidity as dependent variables and socioeconomic status, educational level, ethnic group, or living conditions as independent variables almost constantly show associations or correlations: the more pronounced the social disadvantage, the higher the frequency of affections or hazards and the probability of premature death.[30] However, for this reality to be perceived and interpreted, a major change in the perspective on both health and causality had to occur. Under the new paradigm, health was not only an individual concern any more, it could also be apprehended at a population level; and causality was not necessarily an unequivocal determinism any more, it could better be understood in terms of probability.[31] The social, in all its aspects, had become a risk measured through odds ratios and other indicators that could reveal the statistical effect of a social variable on a physical variable. How much does the risk of disease or death increase with the presence of a so-called risk factor, such as being a blue-collar worker, belonging to a racial minority, having dropped out of high school, or living in a disadvantaged neighborhood? This is the question to which demography and epidemiology now bring possible answers, thus validating Hallbwachs's and Canguilhem's intuitions that a society has the mortality that suits it depending on the value attached to life by its members.

The United States offers a remarkable illustration of this statistical link between the social and the physical due to the depth of its inequalities and the quality of available data. To understand how the wealthiest and most powerful country in the world, with the highest health spending and the most advanced medical technology, came to rank 34th for life expectancy at birth, 42nd for mortality under five, behind Cuba, and, in terms of probability of premature death between the age of 15 and 60, 44th for males, tied with Algeria, and 48th for females, tied with Armenia, one needs to take into account the way the variance of each indicator weighs on the average.

This is a simple arithmetical fact: insofar as the benefits for the most privileged categories are slowing down, the more the data are spread out, the more the average is dropping, with the disadvantaged categories dragging it downwards. Thus, life expectancy at birth is six years less among black men than among white men; the difference is four and a half years for women. In both sexes, between 25 and 64, the death rate is almost twice as high among blacks than among whites. But this is not just a question of color. The gap in life expectancy between the richest 1 percent and the poorest 1 percent is almost 15 years for males and 10 years for females. Combining ethnoracial and sociocultural dimensions, the difference in life expectancy between college-educated whites and black high-school dropouts is 14 years for men and 10 years for women.[32] Considered together, these disparities explain the poor ranking of the country in international comparisons as regards to mortality and life expectancy. However, the processes accounting for these inequalities are complex. They are not limited to the material elements reflecting the socioeconomic level in terms of diet, housing, or occupation. Other factors, both sociological and psychological, of which recent works have established the negative impact, are also crucial, in particular the everyday experience of discrimination and depreciation.[33] To take stock of the inequality of lives, to render it visible and grasp its logics, demographers and epidemiologists must explore its diverse expressions and multiple mechanisms.

Occasionally, however, this inequality is so manifest that it is perceived, at least by its victims, without having to be objectified in statistical studies. This is what the mobilizations around the killings of African American men by the police reveal. Such a social movement was hardly thinkable only a few years earlier. While I was conducting my research on urban policing in the disadvantaged outskirts of Paris, I had several conversations with American researchers who were surprised by the protests and demonstrations that occurred in France each time someone, usually a working-class youth of immigrant origin, was killed as a result of an interaction with the police. According to them, such reactions had no equivalent in their country. In fact, social scientists were even trying to build hypotheses to explain this difference, which was all the more remarkable since such tragic events were frequent in the United States.[34] Then, in the summer of 2014, Michael Brown, a young African American, was shot dead by a white officer in the small town of Ferguson, Missouri, during a banal identity check. While the local protests that followed met with a response of harsh repression from militarized police, the protesters' slogan "Hands up, don't shoot" became a rallying cry all over the country. Three-quarters of the grand jury which had to decide on the indictment of the officer consisted of white citizens, whereas two thirds of the inhabitants of the city and its surroundings were African Americans. Blatantly influenced by a prosecutor who was himself accused of partiality, it concluded that the case did not justify further judicial proceeding, exacerbating the African American community's indignation. Thus, the violent death of the young man, the disproportionate response to the demonstrations, and the impunity the officer benefited from provoked, for the first time in decades, a national reaction under the banner of the Black Lives Matter movement, whose name became the protesters' motto. At the same time, the awareness of the banality of such events grew within the population as the media started reporting, almost on a daily basis, similar incidents during which African American men were shot dead by the police. The hypotheses that had been proposed by social scientists to account for the alleged apathy of the black population and the supposed indifference of society were suddenly invalidated.

In fact, the public's disregard of the problem had something to do with the fact that the deaths occurring in these circumstances were only partially recorded, and never communicated. As a sign that these deaths did not count, they were not seriously counted. Again, statistics were essential to provide the evidence. It took an independent inquiry conducted by British journalists in 2015 to shed light on the gravity of the issue.[35] In 12 months, in the United States, 1,134 deaths had occurred at the hands of law-enforcement officers. During the first 24 days of that year, the toll was higher than that observed in England in similar conditions during the last 24 years. The death rate resulting from these interactions with the police showed that young black men were nine times more likely than other people and five times more likely than white men of the same age to be killed by the police. However, it was difficult to assume that the difference could be due to African Americans being objectively more dangerous than white men since the former were twice as likely not to have a weapon than the latter when they were shot. Certainly, the constitutional right to keep and bear arms and the general level of violence in society, particularly in disadvantaged areas inhabited in majority by African Americans, partially explain these figures. But the impressive number of these homicides in the United States compared to that of England reveals a distinct way of apprehending the value of lives, and the considerable differences between socioracial categories reflect moral hierarchies in the valuation of people.

A case among many others illustrates this dual dimension of the devaluation of lives. In August 2016, a young black man, suspected of drug trafficking, was shot dead by a police officer in Milwaukee.[36] Having seen the latter approaching, he had fled the scene, throwing away his weapon. The police officer had shot him a first time in the arm, which resulted in the young man falling down, then, as the man was lying on the ground his hands above his head, a second time in the chest from a distance of a few inches which caused his death. Protests had followed, leading the Governor of Wisconsin to declare a state of emergency. During the trial, 10 months later, the prosecutor declared that "shooting someone point blank when he's on the ground is utter disregard for life." This was the legal definition of "first-degree reckless homicide," which implied a heavy prison sentence. However, the jury decided otherwise and the officer was acquitted. On the evening after the death of the young man, he had gone to a bar and publicly " 'bragged about being able to do whatever' he wanted 'without repercussions,' " and, to demonstrate it, he had assaulted a customer. Justice seemed to prove him right. Indeed, this is yet another indication of the indifference toward life, or at the very least, certain lives: the lack of consequences when the police kill outside the context of self-defense. In seven years, 41 agents were charged with murder or manslaughter for on-duty shootings, which represents less than 1 percent of all police killings.[37] Indeed, in almost all cases, grand juries decide not to indict them, whereas, by contrast, when ordinary citizens commit homicides, indictment is almost automatic.

However, among African Americans, the experience of discrimination and of devaluation of their lives, which is both revealed by the banality of police violence and the impunity for the perpetrators, goes beyond these tragic events resulting in the death of young men. It is the everyday experience of harassment by law enforcement agents in the street, the disproportionate severity of the justice system, the appalling abuse in correctional facilities, and the humiliation of ordinary racism in the public sphere as well as in interpersonal relations.[38] How little their lives are worth is part of their ordinary experience in their interactions with the authorities and their agents: in the labor

market, their rate of unemployment is higher, the color of
their skin even appearing to be more than criminal records
an obstacle to obtaining a job interview, while for those
employed, salaries are lower than for the rest of the population; in real estate, while excluded from certain areas,
they are, as tenants, at the mercy of inflexible landlords,
and, as homeowners, the victims of unscrupulous bankers,
with the risk of ending up on the streets overnight, as
was the case for hundreds of thousands of them in the
aftermaths of the 2008 subprime mortgage crisis; finally,
in public services, the reduction of spending for common
goods happens to the detriment of the quality of life, as
demonstrated by the 2014 decision by the authorities in
Flint, Michigan, to modify the water source for budget
considerations, thus knowingly exposing the population,
mostly composed of poor blacks, to lead poisoning.[39] The
devaluation of lives, for minorities, especially African
Americans, is the ordinary texture of existence, in which
here and there emerge extraordinary events putting lives
at stake. The outburst of anger is then the expression of
frustrations and humiliations accumulated over the years.

However, it may be necessary to widen the empirical
setting in which one thinks of death. It is not only physical. It can also be social. The concept of social death has
been introduced in relation to slavery as it was practiced
in numerous societies, from ancient Greece to the United
States, as well as the African and Muslim worlds.[40] It is
based on the idea that the individuals reduced to slavery
are desocialized from the group to which they belong and
resocialized in a completely alienated form. They are not
persons any more, but goods that their owner can treat
as they like, which includes the possibility of selling or
killing them. In contemporary societies, where slavery has
not entirely disappeared, captivity represents a normal-
ized form of social death, particularly when it comes to
life imprisonment without parole, since the convict essentially loses his identity, his rights, and his place in society.
Besides, in the same way that enslavement of enemies was

often a way to avoid their execution, long-term sentences frequently represent an alternative to capital punishment. In both cases, a sort of equivalence is established between physical death and social death. With respect to prisoners, certain practices accentuate even more the meaning and experience of this equivalence. It is the case for solitary confinement, which generally corresponds to disciplinary measures internal to the correctional system but sometimes also proceeds from preventive logics regarding individuals considered to be particularly dangerous.[41] In the United States, out of 2.1 million inmates, it is estimated that 150,000 are serving life sentences, a third being without parole, while 80,000 are in solitary confinement, several thousand being kept in isolation for years, even decades, in conditions known to generate psychotic disorders. Regardless of the systems of justification underlying them, these social deaths are extreme expressions of the depreciation of human life. Yet they are not neutral when it comes to the ethnoracial and socioeconomic categories they affect. Poor black men are overrepresented both in prisons for long-term sentences and in solitary confinement units.[42] In a country where the incarcerated population has been multiplied by seven in a little more than three decades, black men are proportionally eight times more represented than white men in prison. One out of three African American male high-school dropouts is behind bars, which is the case for only one in a hundred in the general male population. Two thirds of life imprisonment without parole sentences for non-violent crime are meted out to black men. As for solitary confinement, available data do not allow a differentiation across all correctional facilities, but local statistics indicate a disproportionate presence of African Americans.

If the unequal value of lives can thus be expressed through the disparities before death in the various forms I have discussed, it is still necessary to analyze how social realities are inscribed in the life of human beings, understood in its dual material and experiential dimension, that is, how social facts have an imprint in both the living and the lived. Here, quantitative analysis is not enough. It must be enriched by qualitative approaches. In that regard, ethnography provides invaluable elements of intelligibility. I will mobilize it through the account of the lives of two men with whom I have had numerous interactions in the course of my research in France and in South Africa.

The first one was a young Moroccan who came to France when he was 12.[43] His father, a construction worker, after having gradually consolidated his own material situation, had asked his wife and children to join him. Quickly regularized via the procedure of family reunification, which was then relatively easy, the household lived in a housing project on the outskirts of Paris. Without points of reference in this new environment, the adolescent soon had academic difficulties and eventually dropped out of school. Having been trained as a turner, he was nonetheless unable to get a job. At the time, the economic context was not favorable, unemployment rates were rapidly increasing, and racial discrimination was common on the labor market. Left idle in his neighborhood, he spent his time with other youths experiencing similar situations. He became addicted to heroin, committed various misdemeanors, and ended up being sentenced various times to imprisonment for drug offenses. Between his incarcerations, he managed to find jobs, first on a construction site, then in a warehouse, and finally as a courier, but these were always short-term contracts. At some point, he found out that he was HIV-positive, most probably as a consequence of his heroin addiction. Shortly before, he had appeared in court and been sentenced to what was then called a "double punishment," the incarceration being followed by a deportation. In fact, considering the legislation of that time, he could have applied at the age of 16 for French citizenship but not having done so he had been granted, when he turned 18, a 10-year residence permit – which the judge had rescinded. Henceforth illegally present on the French territory, he could nevertheless not be deported since he was married

to a French woman with whom he had four children, all
with French citizenship. Diseased, undocumented, without
any resources, fearing to be reported if he sought help from
the social or medical services, he lived hidden in a squatted apartment, whose blinds were always closed, with his
wife and children. When he fell sick with a severe form
of tuberculosis, he resigned himself to go to the hospital
under his brother's name. The identity theft was discovered and his medical care interrupted. Back home, he
could not continue his treatment. His medical condition
worsened. When he finally went to see a physician, who
had him immediately admitted, it was too late. He died a
few days later. He was 36.

The second man is a South African born in the rural
north of the country.[44] Like most inhabitants of this region
where the white government had dispossessed black peasants of their lands under the terms of the Native Land Acts
of 1913 and 1936, his father could not find any work in
the wretched homeland where his ethnic group was confined and had to seek employment on the farm of a white
landowner. With his wife and their five children, who were
also gradually put to work, he lived in a small mud house.
There were six other families on the compound. Wages
were low and material conditions poor. When a misde-
meanor was discovered, often a simple pilfering of avoca-
dos or mangoes from the owner's orchards, a public
beating was inflicted on the culprit with a heavy leather
whip like those used by white police officers to quash the
protests against apartheid. One day, having suffered this
humiliating punishment, the 20-year-old son decided to
leave the farm. He settled in the neighboring homeland
created by the regime and found a better-paid, less demand-
ing job as a gardener. Shortly after, he married a young
woman who worked as a maid for a local black family.
However, after several months, the white landowner
needed more labor and demanded that the homeland
administration dismiss him, so he was forced to leave his
wife and return to the farm. Several years later, with the

growing industrialization of the agrobusiness, the property was bought by an international consortium and he was hired by the new company. Now living in a barracks with dozens of male workers, he spent his weekends on the homestead, as his colleagues did, drinking with women from the villages nearby. Once a month, when he received his salary, he sent for his wife. Their two children were raised by their grandparents as their presence was not allowed at their father's or their mother's workplace. The couple ended up separating and, for a while, the man lived with one of the women who was selling beer at weekends. When she fell sick, the landowner brutally dismissed her, accusing her of contaminating his workers. The man fell sick in turn. At the hospital, he was diagnosed with AIDS. He received treatment and his condition somewhat improved. On his return to the farm, however, he was fired. When he insisted on receiving his last salary and a termination payment, his employer threatened him with a rifle. Too weak to find another job, without any means and with no place to reside, the man went to stay with his sister who lived in the area. Unwelcome, ostracized because of his disease, he was relegated to settle alone in a mud house in the backyard, eating the family's leftovers. After two years of this hardship, he was eventually integrated into a government program for diseased persons. The grant he received allowed him to regain financial independence and find a place of his own. Thanks to the medical care by the public hospital, he recovered a taste for life and was able to enjoy it for some time.

These two life stories, which do not differ much from others I collected during my research in France and South Africa, illustrate the process of what can be called the embodiment of inequality, that is, the inscription of an unequal social order into bodies. Beyond their specificities, given their respective contexts, they could easily be compared to other life accounts, such as that told by João Biehl, of a young Brazilian woman suffering from a degenerative neurological disease and abandoned by her family in a hospice named Vita.[45] Regarding the two men, one can trace the stages and modalities of this embodiment of inequality. In the first case, the uprooting of the Moroccan adolescent from the familiar environment of his childhood, his disorientation while settling in a housing project, his school failure, his precarious jobs, his unemployment and idleness combine to create the conditions for, on the one hand, his exposure to drug addiction, which eventually leads to the infection, and, on the other hand, his involvement with criminal networks, which causes him to be sentenced to prison and have his residence permit revoked; hence, the disease and the absence of treatment ultimately result in his death. In the second case, the dispossession of black people's lands by the white ruling class, the working conditions close to serfdom on the traditional farm, where the landowner is able not only to administer his own justice but also to disenfranchise his workers, and the deleterious organization of labor in the large agricultural enterprise, which provokes the separation of couples, the alienation in drinking, and the facilitation of prostitution – as is also the case in the mining industry – contribute to the disruption of conjugal bonds and kinship structures, and increase the hazard of sexually transmitted diseases; hence, the illness and, since the man is deemed worthless, the dismissal, marginalization, and isolation.

Of course, the concept of embodiment does not imply an ineluctable determinism through which the social would simply translate into the biological: not all immigrants in France and not all poor farmworkers in South Africa share the same fate as these two men, although the proportion of those who do is much higher among these categories than among the rest of the population in their respective countries. But in both contexts, the treatment of human beings reflects a politics of life grounded on the unequal worth and unequal dignity of these existences. The state plays a crucial role in this politics. In the first case, immigration laws, ceaselessly revised, allow an additional penalty, deportation being added to imprisonment to the detriment of his medical condition and family life. In the second case, the segregation regime deprives black households of their lands and rights, and render their material conditions so difficult that they are reduced to accepting a form of enslavement and captivity on the farms of white owners.

However, the state can also play a corrective role regarding disparities. A few years after the death of the young Moroccan, two laws were passed in France: one, under a socialist government, rendered possible the regularization of undocumented immigrants suffering from serious health conditions; the other, under a conservative majority, reduced the scope of the double penalty, preventing many from being deported after their prison time. Had he lived longer, the man would probably have benefited from both measures and would perhaps have had a less infelicitous destiny. Similarly, although the end of apartheid in South Africa did not modify substantially the living conditions of the majority of poor peasants in remote areas of the country, as this account illustrates, two policies decided by the democratic regime had a decisive impact for many persons living with AIDS: free treatment for severe diseases and disability grants for seriously ill persons. As a result of both initiatives, the man's condition improved and he recovered some of his lost dignity.

But the laws passed and the measures implemented represent only a portion of the trials and tribulations affecting these biographies. Politics of life do not only depend on state policies. They involve the entire society. These two stories show how, beyond the specifics of each national context, racial discrimination, spatial segregation, economic disparities, and social rejection conjointly contribute to what can be considered a social death, which precedes the biological death. How else could we describe the reclusion of one man in an apartment, with blinds closed, at the heart of a housing project, and the relegation of the other to a mud house, sidelined by his hostile family?

These case studies may seem extreme in terms of the tragic fate of the two men, as well as the possibility of tracing an almost causal link between the social and the biological. But precisely because they exaggerate the traits, they render more evident two facts of general import. First, they lead us to differentiate two sorts of inequality: one by exclusion, the other by exploitation. In the inequality by exclusion, the person is deemed to have no social utility, and may even be seen as having a social cost, his life being worthless for society. In the inequality by exploitation, the person is viewed only as labor force; his life has worth inasmuch as it contributes to the production of wealth. Second, the political economy that produces these two forms of inequality supposes a moral economy. To exclude or to exploit individuals or groups, one needs to justify one's acts toward others and toward oneself. The devaluation of the concerned individuals or groups serves as a justification for the treatment to which they are subjected. Political economy and moral economy are closely linked, but as can be seen in these two cases, the former precedes the latter – or, better, underlies it.

Politics is ultimately an intervention of society upon human lives. For Foucault, it is a fundamental trait of modernity, which he calls "biopolitics." However, by this word, he means the government of populations, as he is more interested in the "how" of this intervention (the technologies of government) than in the "what" (the matter of politics). By changing the phrasing for politics of life, my endeavor was to reassess the relation between politics and life by taking seriously each of these terms. What does politics make of human lives, and how do they treat them? The stake of this reformulation is not only intellectual; it is also political. Answering this question indeed reveals the profound tension between the ethics and the politics of life, between the affirmation of the value of life as supreme good and the inequality of the worth of lives in the real world.

In theory, the idea that life has become invaluable implies that it should not be possible to give it a monetary equivalent. However, legal practices of compensation for homicides and social practices to arrange marriages have for a long time and in various societies implied the determination, more or less formalized or negotiated, of sums and goods supposed to represent the worth of the person, in these cases deceased or married. Although the ethics it claimed was far removed from the reality of its discourses and practices, Christianity played an important role in the initial resistance to the monetarization of lives, as revealed by the ideological battle when life insurance was created. Eventually, the idea that the worth of a life could be quantified and, therefore, that its loss could lead to a compensation imposed itself to the point of being today an international norm, even though its application considerably varies from one country to another, and even from one hazard to another. If the way for compensation of occupational accidents was somewhat paved more than a hundred years ago, the principle was then extended to a series of misfortunes, whether human, natural, or simply unforeseen, and it now implies a collective moral responsibility, resulting in the creation of funds and institutions dedicated to the indemnification of victims. The comparison of sums paid to the families of people deceased in similar circumstances thus reveal disparities, sometimes of considerable proportions, in the allocated amounts or simply in the recognition of the right to compensation. Once given a monetary equivalent, the value of life proves to be ostensibly unequal.

But in principle, life is not only supposedly invaluable; it is also deemed inalienable. Yet, again, a number of ancient or remote societies have practiced servitude, notably for prisoners of war, or serfdom, particularly in feudal societies. As for the modern Western world, it easily accommodated the multiple forms of alienation involved in the slave trade, slavery, colonization, apartheid, and genocides. Ironically, these infamous practices were conducted by nations which proclaimed the universality of human rights, some even invoking divine authority and religious principles. All these systems of domination – to which exploitation, segregation, extermination, and dehumanization measures could be added – were rendered possible by the devaluation of the lives of those who were being subjugated, even eliminated. For the treatment inflicted on the Indians on the American continent, black people in the United States and in South Africa, colonial subjects in the British and French empires to appear acceptable, even desirable, the worth of each of these groups had to be diminished, and their humanity even contested.

Although the most brutal manifestations of domination have declined, even though they always seem to be about to emerge again here and there, some less spectacular expressions of alienation are present in contemporary societies. They are particularly translated in the inequalities before death, between countries as much as within them. These inequalities are often invisible, only revealed by the calculations of statisticians. But they may become patent in the violence committed toward certain groups or categories, sometimes by the very public authorities supposed to protect them. Far from being an unpredictable event, and the product of coincidences and contingencies, death is thus the translation into the bodies of unequal social relations in which history left its mark. What we call life expectancy is its double. The phrase is to be understood in its regular demographic acceptance of average life span, in other words, the inscription of the past in the living. But it should also be apprehended in a philosophical sense, suggesting expectation, in other words, the inscription of the future in the lived. Thus, the inequalities in life expectancy do not simply call for the measure of quantities of life (the average number of years in the existence of individuals), but just as much for the recognition of qualities of life (the self-realization in the relation with others). In their most simple but perhaps also ambitious formulation, politics of life deal with this dual dimension of life expectancy.

Returning from a trip to Germany in 1948, the sociologist Everett Hughes wrote a text in which he pondered over the attitude of the German people toward the Nazi efforts to exterminate Jews: "How could such dirty work be done among and, in a sense, by the millions of ordinary civilized German people?" he asks.[46] He offers a possible answer provided by a casual conversation he had in Frankfurt with an architect who, after having expressed his shame of his fellow countrymen, added nonetheless: "The Jews, they were a problem. They came from the East. You should see them in Poland; the lowest class of people, full of lice, dirty and poor, running about in their ghettos in filthy caftans. They came here, and got rich by unbelievable methods after the first war." It is this ambiguity, this way of distancing himself from the genocide but, at the same time, of implicitly finding justifications for it, that interests Hughes: "Having dissociated himself clearly from these people, and having declared them a problem, he apparently was willing to let someone else do to them the dirty work which he himself would not do, and for which he expressed shame." Rather than mere complicity, this was acting by proxy.

But Hughes does not stop there. It would certainly be comfortable to deem the reaction of the German population under the Nazi regime an aberration of the human condition, he observes, but could we not establish parallels with more familiar situations which proceed from similar rationales, even if we are not ready to admit it? "There are plenty of examples in our own world," he affirms. He mentions in particular the abuse of inmates in United States prisons, which most citizens accept and even often deem legitimate considering that offenders deserve it. For him, it is the crime committed, or supposed so, that diminishes the value of the lives of criminals and justifies their demeaning treatment. But can we limit the analysis to this sole moral dimension? Should we not ask if all offenders are effectively disgraced and degraded in the same way? It is manifestly not the case.[47] The act and the condemnation it provokes are not enough to explain the debasing treatment some are subjected to. Much more determining seem to be the identity of the offenders and the way they are represented. In the same manner as the architect did not denigrate the Jews because they were poor and ragged and had become wealthy and arrogant, but because they were Jews, those who depreciate poor black prisoners and prove themselves indifferent to their fate in prison do so not only because of the wrong for which these inmates have been sentenced but also by reason of their being poor and black. "The greater their social distance from us, the more we leave in the hands of others a sort of mandate by default to deal with them on our behalf," Hughes notes – and this allows us "not to know," in particular when appalling acts are committed against them.

Evidence of it can be found in the way those who attempt to reach Europe, fleeing persecutions, war, or destitution, are treated, since they are not suspected of having committed any crime. Whereas 30,000 persons have died since 2000 while trying to cross the Mediterranean Sea, the European Union's response has been to replace the rescue system it had initially imagined, Mare Nostrum, by what is essentially a police operation, Triton, which has rendered the crossing even more perilous, and to delegate to authoritarian or anomic states, such as Turkey or Libya, where human rights violations are well documented, the task of containing and repressing the flow of refugees and migrants. In March 2011, a boat carrying 72 Africans drifted, out of fuel, for 14 days off the coast of Tripoli, their distress calls not being answered.[48] Monitored by NATO radars, approached by ships and overflown by helicopters, the boat eventually ran aground. Only 11 migrants had survived, two of them dying shortly after. Their "distance from us," in Hughes's words, was probably experienced as being too great. The decision not to rescue these human beings suggests that their existence was deemed not worth such an attempt, and reminds us that politics of life are always politics of inequality.

Conclusion
Unequal Lives

All the dead voices ... – What do they say? – They talk
about their lives. – To have lived is not enough for them.
– They have to talk about it.

> Samuel Beckett, *Waiting for Godot*, 1954 [1952]

At the end of this investigation, one question insistently
remains: where exactly is the "true life" that Adorno
declares must be mourned, in *Minima Moralia*? One of
Arthur Rimbaud's most frequently quoted lines appears
to offer an elusive response to this question: "The true
life is elsewhere." The problem is that this phrase, so
often reproduced in both scholarly works and encyclope-
dia articles, is apocryphal. In fact, in *A Season in Hell*, the
19-year-old poet wrote: "The true life is absent."[1] Perhaps
it is because of his far-flung peregrinations in Aden and
Abyssinia that Rimbaud is imagined to be seeking life
"elsewhere" – this life which in reality his "foolish virgin"
says is "absent," adding: "We are not in the world."
Nearly a century later, Emmanuel Lévinas takes up this
enigmatic utterance at the beginning of *Totality and Infinity*. But he reorients it through a syntactical inversion:
" 'The true life is absent.' But we are in the world."[2] And
he continues, in sibylline fashion: "Metaphysics arises and

is maintained in this alibi." Metaphysics is born, according to Lévinas, in the movement between "a world that
is familiar to us" and "an alien outside-of-oneself," and
hence derives from a radical search for alterity: "The
metaphysical desire tends toward something else entirely,
toward the absolutely other." In this sense it is transcendent, striving to bridge the divide between an absence and
a presence, between life and the world. The final fragment
of Adorno's text also seems oriented toward a similar transcendence:[3] "Perspectives must be fashioned that displace
and estrange the world, reveal it to be, with its rifts and
crevices as indigent and distorted as it will one day appear
in the messianic light." But this is an "utterly impossible thing", he adds immediately, because it "presupposes
a standpoint removed, even though by a hair's breadth,
from the scope of existence." We find ourselves, then,
at an impasse.

The reflection I have tried to develop in this book began
from a comparable interrogation of the tension, expressed
by Lévinas and in more somber tone by Adorno, between
the supposed eclipse of life and the affirmed evidence of
our presence in the world. But it has not been conducted
via metaphysics: throughout this inquiry, I have been considering physical life and physical presence. The otherness
I am interested in has nothing to do with transcendence:
it is the otherness of the Syrian refugee and the Zimbabwean asylum-seeker, of the young Palestinian mother and
the Kurdish hunger striker, of the undocumented Algerian
patient and the sick South African farmworker. And this
otherness does not imply a radical absolute: it is manifested in everyday relations as revealed in the treatment
of precarious lives, endangered lives, discriminated lives.
In short, it is a matter not of the abstract yet normative
representation of the "face in which the Other – the absolutely other – presents himself," as Lévinas puts it, but
of facts that call for a description and an interpretation
linked to concrete situations: a camp in Calais and a district of Johannesburg, administrative decisions concerning

seriously ill migrants in France and the care given in Israel to a child from Gaza, marriages between disabled people in Senegal and police killings of young black men in the United States. Rather than a metaphysics of alterity, what is at stake is a physics of inequality – as is attested by the fact that the biological and biographical dimensions are tightly bound in forms of life, and that ethics of life cannot be thought independently of politics of life.

In adopting the perspective I have taken in this book, placing the issue of inequality at the heart of the inquiry, I do not account for all the elements that make up life. I have left aside the esthetic aspect, that of arts of living and lifestyles, aware of the attention legitimately devoted to them by others.[4] I have deliberately ignored cultural considerations as they have been applied to consumer society and scenarios of the future.[5] I have been less concerned with life stories than with forms of life, less with notions of what constitutes a good life than with the ethics that construct life as a supreme good, less with ways of governing human lives than with the politics through which societies express the differential values of these lives. What I have sought to understand is life as it brings into play both the moral and the political economies of our time, as it is put into play in the contemporary world – "life itself" as it "has become a problem," to use Nietzsche's phrase.[6] For that reason, as I indicated in the preamble, I have prioritized coherence over an impossible exhaustiveness. Reflecting on the question of unequal lives has seemed to me a more urgent theoretical and practical imperative than elaborating an improbable anthropology of life – an exercise on which others have ventured in ways that have not been truly convincing.

This choice has two important implications, which mark a twofold rupture with many anthropological, sociological, and philosophical works. Indeed, speaking about inequality represents an invitation to analyze the whole of the social world, not merely its lower sectors, but to do so relationally and differentially, not as a homogeneous whole. Thus, on the one hand, the point is not to isolate the lives of the exiled, the oppressed, the exploited, the humiliated, and the wronged, at the risk of promoting a miserabilist reading, but to insert them into social relations whose fundamental injustice resides precisely in an implicitly established or explicitly acknowledged hierarchy of lives. It is this hierarchy that allows them to be inferiorized, stigmatized, and brutalized while other lives are privileged. And on the other hand, the question is not to reflect on the generic traits of contemporary societies, as is often done for the purposes of condemning their individualism, their consumerism, their punitive turn, the ubiquity of surveillance, and the empire of the spectacle, while underestimating the disparities manifested within these sociological tendencies and their differential effects on the lives of individuals. The issue is precisely the unequal distribution of consequences that enables the production and reproduction of these generic traits.

To paraphrase Bourdieu, lives are not characterized only by their "condition"; they need also to be understood in terms of their "position."[7] The life of the "have-nots," whether they lack documents, home, citizenship, land, or rights, can only be understood in relation to the life of the "haves," those who benefit from these prerogatives that are generally taken for granted, and this relationship is mediated by the whole range of institutions that contribute to legitimizing and maintaining these disparities. Limiting the investigation to the bottom of the social scale is no more satisfactory than approaching society from a merely homogenizing perspective. Considering life through the lens of inequality thus makes the social world intelligible anew, but also offers new possibilities for intervention. It enables us to move from expressing compassion to recognizing injustice.

The decision to address life from the point of view of inequality does not derive purely from a theoretical and practical imperative: it is also an ethical and political imperative. For those who live in the situations I have studied do not suffer only through their many privations. They also suffer because their alienation is not named as such. In that respect, the reality of unequal lives is not a new discovery made by the social scientist: it is an integral component of the awareness of those who are on the wrong side of inequality, even if it is usually ignored, hidden, or contested by the others. This awareness is manifested through multifarious forms of protest which are all too rarely acknowledged: refugees who sew their lips together in a French camp and prisoners who crucify themselves in an Ecuadorian prison, young Palestinians who attack soldiers of the occupying army, and activists of the Black Lives Matter movement who protest against the killing of African Americans by police officers. But it is more often expressed surreptitiously and invisibly, in the private space of conversations with family or friends, or even in interviews with a journalist or encounters with an ethnographer.

Over the course of my research in sub-Saharan Africa, Latin America, and France, I have often heard, voiced with varying degrees of openness, this discourse condemning both injustice and the denial of injustice. It was notably expressed to me by young men from working-class backgrounds and ethnoracial minorities in the Paris region, whom I saw continually harassed, insulted, and bullied by law enforcement agents in their neighborhood, and whom I sometimes met again in prison after they were incarcerated following summary court proceedings during which they were abused, denigrated, and belittled by the magistrates.[8] Indeed, the "struggle for recognition," whose grammar is the subject of Axel Honneth's study, is indissociable from its negative counterpart, "the experience of humiliation or disrespect."[9] Consequently, the most basic recognition owed to those who bear the weight of the inequality of lives is to recognize not only this reality, of which they are the victims and which they experience daily, but also the consistent denial of it, a denial of which they themselves are acutely aware. It is in this sense that the "user's manual" evoked in the title of this book can be claimed as critical.

An opposition is commonly drawn between two lines of critical thought.[10] The first one, epitomized by Marx and Horkheimer, holds that we are prisoners of an ideology that prevents us from seeing the world as it is: the work of critique therefore consists in freeing ourselves by exposing this alienation, that is to say the logics, interests, and powers that obstruct analysis of our condition – though the dominated demonstrate social intelligence more often than this theory supposes. The second one, exemplified by Nietzsche and Wittgenstein, asserts that we are captives of a view of things that gives them a false appearance of self-evidence: in this case the work of critique is to become aware of the arbitrary and contingent character of our values, norms, and representations, in other words to question what the force of habit and the weight of conformism makes us take for granted – but here too the dominated may prove more perceptive than is commonly believed.[11] The first line, normative, held by the Frankfurt School, leads to social critique: our task is to change the world. The second line, genealogical, developed by Foucault, leads to cognitive critique: our task is to change our view on the world.

By analyzing how, in societies deemed democratic, the valuation of abstract life as supreme good does not prevent the differential evaluation of concrete lives, how the international duty to protect lives exposed to deadly danger does not preclude the relentless repression of those thus endangered, how the humanitarian principle of saving lives does not rule out the martyrdom principle of sacrificing one's life for a cause, and more broadly by examining the unequal treatment of lives, I hope to have shown that the two critiques are not incompatible and that changing our perspective on the world is even a prerequisite to changing it. Certainly, exposing the contradictions that run through the moral economy of life does not make contemporary societies any more equitable, but it does offer weapons to those who wish to fight for greater justice. At a time when disparities are deepening, when discourses of exclusion and practices of discrimination are becoming routine, when the marginalization of individuals and groups on the basis of their social background, skin color, faith, origin, or gender is expressed more and more openly, and when, in addition, lie and deception are increasingly viewed as instruments for the conquest and exercise of power, critique does not have to choose between militancy and lucidity, between contesting misleading ideologies and challenging false self-evidence. Revealing and elucidating what the unequal treatment of human lives signifies and implies is a matter of both intellectual and political engagement, which the work of critique should, modestly but firmly, claim.

Notes

Preamble: *Minima Theoria*

1 See Theodor Adorno (1974 [1951]: 15).

2 See Rahel Jaeggi (2005: 66–8) on the critical aspect of Adorno's understanding of form of life.

3 See W. H. Auden (2011 [1947]), whose poem deals with the distress of his time.

4 See Miguel Abensour (1982), whose article has been republished as a postface of the French version of *Minima Moralia*.

5 See the two seminal articles by Edward Palmer Thompson (1971) and Lorraine Daston (1995), as well as my essay (Fassin 2009c) and our collective volume (Fassin and Jean-Sébastien Eideliman 2012), which offers a reformulation of the concept and provide a series of case studies conducted on several continents.

6 See John Locke (1836 [1689]: 369), for whom the term "life" epitomizes the "misuse of words" due to the false impression people have that everyone shares the same understanding of them.

7 See the entry "Life" in the *Encyclopaedia Universalis* (Canguilhem 1990).

8 See the chapter she dedicates to labor, which constitutes with work and action what she names *vita activa* (Arendt 1998 [1958]): 97).

9 See Thomas Khurana (2013: 11) on "the freedom of life" in Hegel's theory.

10 The lectures delivered by Erwin Schrödinger (1944) in Dublin have preceded James Watson and Francis Crick's discovery by a few years.

11 It is the argument developed by Paul Rabinow and Carlo Caduff (2006) against the commonly accepted idea of a molecularization of biology.

12 See, among many, the articles by Madeline Weiss et al. (2016), "The Physiology and Habitat of the Last Universal Common Ancestor," *Nature Microbiology* 1 (July 25), available at: <doi:10.1038/nmicrobiol.2016.116>, and by Sara Seager et al. (2016), "Toward a List of Molecules as Potential Biosignature Gases for the Search of Life on Exoplanets and Applications to Terrestrial Biochemistry," *Astrobiology* 16/6: 465–85.

13 See Heather Keenleyside (2012) on the affinities between John Locke's theory and Laurence Stern's novel.

14 See Marcel Proust (1996 [1927]: 254) in the final volume, *Time Regained*, of *In Search of Lost Time*.

15 See the two classics, in sociology by William Thomas and Florian Znaniecki (1996 [1920]) and in anthropology by Oscar Lewis (1961).

16 For a review of this moment when life stories abounded in anthropological writings, see Gelya Frank (1995).

17 For examples of such a dilemma about the biographies and lives of slaves in the United States, see Saidiya Hartman (2008) and David Kazanjian (2016).

18 See Samuel Beckett's novel *Molloy* (1955 [1951]) and Pierre Bourdieu's article "The Biographical Illusion" (1987 [1986]).

19 See Hannah Arendt (1998 [1958]) and Giorgio Agamben (1998 [1995]).

20 For a critical review of this theory and of its political developments, see Nitzan Lebovic (2006).

21 In a considerable literature, see in particular the collective volume by Sarah Franklin and Margaret Lock (2003), as well as the monographs by Paul Rabinow (1999) on the French deciphering of the genome, Duana Fullwiley (2011) on the Senegalese biologies of sickle cell anemia, Stefan Helmreich (1998) on the digital world of Silicon Valley, and Nikolas Rose (2007) on the biomedically induced transformations in subjectivities.

22 To limit the list to those mentioned here, see the works of Nancy Scheper-Hughes (1992), Bhrigupati Singh (2015), Lucas Bessire (2014), Lisa Stevenson (2014), Michael Jackson (2011), and Zoë Wool (2015).

23 One can cite the studies gathered by Joëlle Vailly, Janina Kehr and Jörg Niewöhner (2011), Marcia Inhorn and Emily Wentzell (2012), and João Biehl and Adriana Petryna (2013).

24 See Tim Ingold's article (2010) on "Walking, Breathing, Knowing," and his collection of texts (2011) significantly titled *Being Alive*.

25 See Eduardo Kohn's article (2007) on "How Dogs Dream," and his sequel (2013) in larger format, *How Forests Think*.
26 See the mostly programmatic article by Perig Pitrou (2014).
27 See Veena Das and Clara Han's (2016) *Living and Dying in the Contemporary World*.
28 See Georges Perec (1987 [1978]: xv).
29 This question has been developed in my inquiry into "The Parallel Lives of Philosophy and Anthropology" (Fassin 2014).
30 See Philip Lewis (1985) on the paradoxes of translation.
31 See George Steiner (1975) on the four moments of the translation.

Chapter I. Forms of Life

1 Originally published in the *Revue de métaphysique et de morale*, it was included in *The Essential Foucault* (Foucault 2003a [1985]: 6–17), from which the quotations are drawn.
2 See his book on the *Knowledge of Life* (Canguilhem 2008 [1952]: xvii–xviii), and, 16 years later, his article on the "new knowledge of life" (Canguilhem 1994 [1968]: 335–7).
3 The five occurrences are noted, as per editorial standard, 19, 23, 241, PPF 1, 345 (Wittgenstein 2009 [1953]).
4 See Lynne Rudder Baker's article (2008: 278).
5 See Kathleen Emmett's article (1990: 213).
6 See Jonathan Lear's text on transcendental anthropology (1986: 272).
7 See Bernard Williams's conference on solipsism and idealism (1974: 84).
8 Initially published in *The Philosophical Review*, the article was later included in a collection (Cavell 1962: 74).
9 In a posthumous collection (Wittgenstein 1998 [1977]).
10 See Canguilhem (1994 [1968]: 335) and Wittgenstein (2009 [1953]: 19).
11 See, for example, the works of John Hartigan (2014) on the multispecies approach and of Veena Das (2006) on violence.
12 See Cavell's conferences on Wittgenstein, in which the former reinterprets the latter in light of Emerson and Thoreau (1989: 40–4).
13 This study constitutes the first part of the fourth volume of *Homo Sacer* (Agamben 2013 [2011]: xi, 96, and 110). The following quotation is from *Means Without End* (Agamben 2000 [1996]: 3–4).
14 See James Laidlaw's (1995) and Saba Mahmood's (2005) classic monographs.

15 In their influential work on the omnipresence of the law in people's lives, however, Patricia Ewick and Susan Silbey (1998) show that this omnipresence does not affect all individuals similarly.

16 See Giorgio Agamben's (2016 [2014]: 207 and 208) *The Use of Bodies.*

17 The series of articles dedicated to forms of life, in the periodical *Raisons politiques*, particularly the contribution of Albert Ogien (2015) and the book by Anne Lovell, Stefania Pandolfo, Veena Das, and Sandra Laugier (2013) on "collective distress" are in this regard exemplary.

18 See the investigation of Calais Migrant Solidarity, *Death at the Calais Border*, available at: <https://calaismigrantsolidarity.wordpress.com/deaths-at-the-calais-border/>.

19 See the study of the Refugee Rights Data Project, *The Long Wait*, available at: <http://refugeerights.org.uk/wp-content/uploads/2016/06/RRDP_TheLongWait.pdf>.

20 See the study in which I show how a surprising dialectic of compassion and repression takes place in the management of these populations (Fassin 2005).

21 See the UNHCR report, *Mid-Year Trends 2015* (Geneva, 2016, available at: <http://www.unhcr.org/en-us/statistics/unhcrstats/56701b969/mid-year-trends-june-2015.html>.

22 See the report of African Centre for Migration & Society, *All Roads Lead to Rejection: Persistent Bias and Incapacity in South African Refugee Status Determination* (Johannesburg, 2012), available at: <http://www.migration.org.za/newcms/uploads/docs/report-35.pdf>, established by the jurist Roni Amit.

23 The research has been conducted in the devastated buildings of Johannesburg's Central Business District and in a camp on the outskirts of the city, as well as with civil servants of the Department of Home Affairs (Fassin, Wilhelm-Solomon, and Segatti 2017).

24 See her study of ordinary vulnerability (Laugier 2015).

25 See her analysis of precarious life (Butler 2004).

26 Some notable examples are the works of Rhacel Parrenas (2001), Seth Holmes (2013), and Kristin Surak (2013).

27 See the UNHCR report, *Mid-Year Trends 2016* (Geneva, 2017), available at: <http://www.unhcr.org/en-us/statistics/unhcrstats/58aa8f247/mid-year-trends-june-2016.html>.

28 Michael Marrus (2002) wrote a history of European refugees in the first half of the twentieth century.

29 For Hannah Arendt (1996 [1943]: 115 and 119), "refugees driven from country to country represent the vanguard of their peoples – if they keep their identity."

30 See Walter Benjamin (1968 [1942]: 257–8).

Chapter II. Ethics of Life

1 This is what John Torpey (1986) suggests. See Max Horkheimer (1972).

2 As Matthew King reminds us (2009). See Habermas (1990 [1985]).

3 This 10-page text constitutes the third part of the introduction to *The Use of Pleasure*, Foucault (1985 [1984]).

4 On moral anthropology, one can consult my edited volume (Fassin 2012), especially the introduction "Toward a Critical Moral Anthropology," and our critical anthology (Fassin and Lézé 2014), particularly the introduction "The Moral Question in Anthropology."

5 The most substantial text is the conference on Émile Durkheim (1974 [1906]), "The Determination of Moral Facts," in *Sociology and Philosophy*, trans. D. F. Pocock (Abingdon: Routledge), esp. pp. 16–26.

6 See the two volumes Edward Westermarck (1906) dedicated to moral ideas, and the collective work edited by Signe Howell (1997) on local moralities.

7 See the books by Lila Abu-Lughod (1986) and Joel Robbins (2004).

8 These concepts are referred to as the "moral problematization of pleasures" (Foucault 1985 [1984]: 26–31 and 63–5).

9 See the research of Talal Asad (1993), James Faubion (2001), Jarrett Zigon (2011), and James Laidlaw (2014).

10 See the texts on ordinary ethics collected by Veena Das (2006) and by Michael Lambek (2015).

11 See my contribution to the book co-authored with Michael Lambek, Veena Das, and Webb Keane (Fassin 2015b), as well as our introduction.

12 According to Max Weber (1994 [1919]), the ethics of conviction focuses on the principles whereas the ethics of responsibility considers above all the foreseeable consequences.

13 Hegel (1991 [1820]) develops its foundations in his *Elements of the Philosophy of Right*.

14 In the chapter he dedicates to "a formal conception of ethical life" (Honneth 1995 [1992]: 172–3).

15 See the discussion between Nancy Fraser and Axel Honneth (2003).

16 This is the radical starting point of Nietzsche, *On the Genealogy of Morals* (1989 [1887]: 19).

17 For a history of immigration in France during this period, see in particular Ralph Schor's book (1996: 248–84).

18 A chapter titled "Compassion Protocol" is dedicated to this measure in my book on the same theme (Fassin 2011: 83–108).

19 These statistics come from documents of the Comité médical pour les exilés, *Rapport d'activité et d'observation 2006* (Kremlin-Bicêtre: Comede, 2007); and of the Office Français de Protection des Réfugiés et des Apatrides, *Rapport d'activité 2005* (Fontenay-sous Bois: Ofpra, 2006), available at: <https://ofpra.gouv.fr/sites/default/files/atoms/files/rapport_dactivite_2005.pdf>.

20 According to the figures released that year by the Office Français de Protection des Réfugiés et des Apatrides, *Rapport d'activité 2001* (Fontenay-sous Bois: Ofpra, 2002), available at: <https://ofpra.gouv.fr/sites/default/files/atoms/files/rapport_dactivite_2001.pdf>.

21 See the study conducted by Dominique Delettre, *Le Maintien des étrangers pour raison médicale sur le territoire français* (Mémoire de Médecin Inspecteur de Santé Publique, Promotion 1998/2000, Rennes, 1999), available at: <http://documentation.ehesp.fr/memoires/1999/misp/delettre.pdf>.

22 The twofold crisis, epidemiological and epistemological, caused by AIDS in South Africa is the subject of the monograph *When Bodies Remember: Experiences and Politics of AIDS in South Africa* (Fassin 2007b [2006]).

23 These figures come from a series of official documents: Joint United Program on HIV/AIDS, *AIDS Epidemic Update: December 2000* (Geneva: UNAIDS/WHO, 2000), available at: <http://data.unaids.org/publications/irc-pub05/aidsepidemicreport2000_en.pdf>; Department of Health, *National HIV and Syphilis Antenatal Sero-Prevalence Survey in South Africa 2002* (Pretoria: RSA, 2002), available at: <http://www.gov.za/sites/www.gov.za/files/hivsyphilis_0.pdf>; Rob Dorrington et al., *The Impact of HIV/AIDS on Adult Mortality in South Africa* (Cape Town: Medical Research Council, 2001), available at: <http://www.mrc.ac.za/bod/complete.pdf>.

24 See data presented by Murray Leibbrandt, Laura Poswell, Pranushka Naidoo, and Matthew Welch (2006).

25 See Giorgio Agamben (1998 [1995]: 1, and 2009 [2008]).

26 In reference to the concept of biopower, i.e. the power on life (Foucault 1978 [1976]), I have proposed the concept of biolegitimacy, i.e. the legitimacy granted to life as supreme good (Fassin 2009a).

27 To account for this phenomenon, Adriana Petryna (2002: 5–7) talks about biological citizenship.

28 See Walter Benjamin's "Critique of Violence" (1986 [1920]: 299), and Hannah Arendt's *On Revolution* (1990 [1963]: 54).

29 See Walter Benjamin's "Critique of Violence" (1986 [1920]): 298–9), and Hannah Arendt's *The Human Condition* (1998 [1958]: 313–14).

30 See the article "Permanence of the Theologico-Political?" by Claude Lefort (1991 [1981]).

31 This spectacular protest, both the expression of a suffering and the performance of a redemption, was the subject of a study by Chris Garces (2012).

32 For an analysis of the dilemmas and the aporias of humanitarianism, refer to my article (Fassin 2007a).

33 See the manifesto by Jean-Hervé Bradol (2004 [2003]: 22), the introduction to a collective work on situations of war.

34 See Peter Singer's book (2009: 15–16), simultaneously published in English and in French under the title *The Life You Can Save: Acting Now to End World Poverty*.

35 See Mark Duffield's study (2001) of global governance in context of war.

36 This research on the non-governmental organizations in the Palestinian Territories was reported in an article (Fassin 2008).

37 Consult the reports written by Médecins sans Frontières and Trapped by War: *The Palestinian Chronicles* (Paris: MSF, 2002), available at: <http://www.doctorswithoutborders.org/sites/usa/files/palestine_09-2002.pdf>; and Médecins du Monde, *Les Civils israéliens et palestiniens victimes d'un conflit sans fin* (Paris: MdM, 2003).

38 Lori Allen's research (2013) is in this regard revealing.

39 The movie by Shlomi Eldar, *Precious Life*, produced by Ehud Bleiberg and Yoav Ze'evi (2010), has been the subject of a specific study (Fassin 2014).

40 In the introduction, he explains his intention: "The general thought I have pursued is that however much we try to distinguish between morally good and morally evil ways of killing, our attempts are beset with contradictions, and these contradictions remain a fragile part of our modern subjectivity" (Asad 2007: 2 and 67).

41 In response to this biosovereignty, Banu Bargu (2014: 328) suggests we talk about a "necroresistance," a form of struggle to death against power.

42 On these boundaries of morality, one can read a series of studies on what we called "the construction of the intolerable" (Fassin and Bourdelais 2005).

43 This ethics of survival was addressed in an article which delves further into the argument of a communication I had delivered during a tribute paid to Jacques Derrida by the École des hautes études en sciences sociales on December 11, 2004, a few weeks after his death (Fassin 2010).

44 Initially published on August 19, 2004, in *Le Monde*, this interview was later translated as *Learning to Live Finally* (Derrida 2007 [2004]: 26).

45 Of his experience in a concentration camp, Robert Antelme (1957 [1947]): 10–11 and 101–2) wrote: "Our objective became the humblest. It was only to survive ... The calling into question of the fact of being human causes a reaction, almost biological, of belonging to the human species."

Chapter III. Politics of Life

1 See Foucault (1985 [1984]: 139).

2 In this regard, reference can be made to the chapter on the "gouvernement de la vie," in *L'Espace politique de la santé* (Fassin 1996).

3 See Foucault (2003b [1997]: 245; 2007 [2004]: 1; 2008 [2004]: 22 and 317).

4 In this "introduction" to the Foucauldian concept, Thomas Lemke (2011) does not only focus on this literature review: he also enriches it with his own contribution to an analysis of biopolitics.

5 In *Bios*, Roberto Esposito (2008 [2004]: 44–6) proposes to "fill" a "semantic void" of the Foucauldian theory of biopolitics by introducing the concept of immunity, which refers both to medicine and law, and more specifically, in both cases to "the power to preserve life."

6 This passage is all the more remarkable since it is well known that Foucault had ambiguous relations with Marxism (1978 [1976]: 140–1).

7 See Ferenc Fehér and Agnes Heller (1994), and Giorgio Agamben (1998 [1995]).

8 See the developments on "the victory of the *animal laborans*" (Arendt 1998 [1958]: 320–5).

9 See Paul Rabinow's and Nikolas Rose's (2006) discussion on this theme.

10 English makes it possible to distinguish between *value*, the quality and desirability of something or someone, and *worth*, the measure of this quality, its quantification, and it is thus possible to differentiate "the value of life" and "the worth of lives" (Fassin 2016).

11 See Thomas Schelling (1984).

12 See Georg Simmel (1978 [1907]: 355–6 and 358).

13 See, for example, Rudolph Peters (2006).

14 Considering only the classics, we can think of Claude Lévi-Strauss (1969 [1949]), for anthropology, and Theodore Schultz (1974), for economics.

15 The research focused both on the economic practices and matrimonial strategies of deaf-mute, blind, paralyzed, and amputated

individuals, as well as persons suffering from malformations – all elements which cause the affected person to be "diminished," as the expression goes in most languages of Senegal (Fassin 1991).

16 This article is a pioneering work in comparative ethics (Read 1955).

17 See the *Evangelium Vitae To the Bishops, Priests and Deacons, Men and Women Religiously Faithful and all People of Good Will on the Value and Inviolability of Human Life* (1995), available at: <http://w2.vatican.va/content/john-paul-ii/en/encyclicals/documents/hf_jp-ii_enc_25031995_evangelium-vitae.html>.

18 See Reinhart Koselleck (2004 [1979]: 169–80).

19 See Viviana Zelizer (2011: 19–39).

20 See Ginger Thompson, "South Africa to Pay $3,900 to Each Family of Apartheid Victims," *The New York Times*, April 16, 2003.

21 The inversion of the moral status of trauma from object of suspicion to object of compassion at the end of the twentieth century is an important symptom of this recognition of victims (Fassin and Rechtman 2009 [2007]).

22 In a memoir, Kenneth Feinberg (2005) has related, sometimes with a certain self-indulgence, his experience of managing the fund. See also Bill Marsh, "Putting a Price on the Priceless: One Life," *The New York Times*, September 9, 2007.

23 See American Civil Liberties Union, *ACLU Releases Files on Civilian Casualties in Afghanistan and Iraq*, April 12, 2007, available at: <https://www.aclu.org/news/aclu-releases-files-civilian-casualties-afghanistan-and-iraq?redirect=cpredirect/29316>; Kenneth Reich, "Soldier's Benefits Could Exceed $800,000," *Los Angeles Times*, April 5, 2003; iCasualties, *Iraq Coalition Casualties: Fatalities By Year*, available at: <http://icasualties.org/iraq/ByYear.aspx>; Amy Hagopian, Abraham Flaxman, Tim Takaro et al., "Mortality in Iraq with the 2003–2011 War and Occupation," *PLOS Medicine*, available at: <http://journals.plos.org/plosmedicine/article?id=10.1371/journal.pmed.1001533>.

24 See Maurice Halbwachs (1913: 94–7).

25 See Georges Canguilhem (1991 [1966]: 161).

26 See Charters of Freedom, *Declaration of Independence of the Thirteen United States of America* (1776), available at: <https://www.archives.gov/founding-docs/declaration-transcript>; Thomas Jefferson, *Original Rough Draft of the Declaration of Independence* (Washington, DC, Library of Congress, 1776), available at: <https://www.loc.gov/exhibits/declara/ruffdrft.html>. The condemnation of slavery in writing did not prevent the third President of the United States from finding arrangements in practice as he owned 175 slaves whom, unlike George Washington, he never freed. See Paul

Finkelman's article ironically titled "The Monster of Monticello," available at: <http://www.nytimes.com/2012/12/01/opinion/the-real-thomas-jefferson.html>.

27 See Jean-Jacques Rousseau's (1985 [1754]: 77) response to the question asked by the Academy of Dijon about "the origin of inequality."

28 In this article, Lorraine Daston (2008) thus opposes the "Babylonian lottery" of Jorge Luis Borges's short story and the "veil of ignorance" of John Rawls's theory of justice, the former maximizing the role of chance, the latter minimizing it.

29 The title of William Coleman's (1982) pioneering book, *Death is a Social Disease*, echoes this important counterintuitive discovery of the first half of the nineteenth century.

30 On social inequalities in health, various works can be consulted (Leclerc et al. 2000; Fassin 2009d).

31 The emergence of statistical and probabilistic thinking in the nineteenth century has been studied by Theodore Porter (1988) and by Ian Hacking (1990).

32 These data are extracted from various epidemiological studies (David Williams et al. 2010; Raj Chetty et al. 2016; Jay Olshansky et al. 2012).

33 It is Nancy Krieger (2000) who provided the first overview of the relations between racial discrimination and health.

34 For a comparison of riots in France and in the United States, see Cathy Lisa Schneider's book (2014), and my article (Fassin 2015a).

35 See John Swaine, Oliver Laughland, Jamiles Lartey, and Ciara McCarthy, "Young Black Men Killed by US Police at Highest Rate in Year of 1,134 Deaths," *Guardian*, December 31, 2015; Jamiles Lartey, "By the Numbers: US Police Kill More in Days than Other Countries do in Years," *Guardian*, June 9, 2015.

36 See Kay Nolan and Julie Bosman, "Milwaukee Officer is Acquitted in Killing of Sylville Smith," *The New York Times*, June 22, 2017.

37 See Zusha Elinson and Joe Palazzolo, "Police Rarely Criminally Charged for On-Duty Shootings," *The Wall Street Journal*, November 24, 2014.

38 In an increasing literature, mention can be made of the works by Victor Rios (2011), Alice Goffman (2014), Laurence Ralph (2014), and, written as a testimony, by Ta-Nehisi Coates (2015).

39 Among a wide variety of works on these themes, one can cite the books by Douglas Massey (2007) and Matthew Desmond (2016), as well as, on the Flint Water Crisis, the article by Mona Hanna-Attisha et al. (2016).

40 The concept of social death has been theorized by Orlando Patterson (1982) as regards to slavery in the United States, and by Claude Meillassoux (1986) as regards to slavery in Africa.

41 The most systematic study of solitary confinement is that of a philosopher, Lisa Guenther (2013).

42 On what is called mass incarceration, see the works by Bruce Western (2006), Michelle Alexander (2010), and Marie Gottschalk (2015). See also the article by Margo Schlanger (2013) and the report by Jennifer Turner and Jamil Dakwar (2014), *Racial Disparities in Sentencing*, Hearing on Reports of Racism in the Justice System of the United States, Inter-American Commission on Human Rights, October 27, 2014, available at: <https://www.aclu.org/sites/default/files/assets/141027_iachr_racial_disparities_aclu_submission_0.pdf>.

43 His story was told in the article entitled "Une double peine" (Fassin 2001).

44 This story is recounted in "A Violence of History" (Fassin 2009b).

45 The institution where the young woman, Catarina, is relegated is described by João Biehl (2005) as a "zone of social abandonment."

46 This article (Hughes 1962: 4–8) led to the concept of "dirty job."

47 This analysis is developed in my book on punishment (Fassin 2018 [2017c]).

48 See Forensic Architecture, *The Left-to-Die Boat*, available at: <http://www.forensic-architecture.org/case/left-die-boat/>.

Conclusion: Unequal Lives

1 See Arthur Rimbaud (2004 [1873]). The French sentence is: "La vraie vie est absente." Among others, Gil Anidjar (2011) uses the apocryphal phrase in his article on "The Meaning of Life," as also does, remarkably, the author of the entry dedicated to the poet in the online *Encyclopédie Larousse*, available at: <http://www.larousse.fr/encyclopedie/personnage/Arthur_Rimbaud/141035>.

2 See Emmanuel Lévinas (1979 [1961]: 33 and 203).

3 See Theodor Adorno (1974 [1951]: 247).

4 See the essays by Alexander Nehamas (1998) and by Marielle Macé (2016).

5 See the works of Zygmunt Bauman (2007) and Marc Abélès (2010 [2006]).

6 In his *The Gay Science* (Nietzsche 2001 [1882]: 7).

7 See Pierre Bourdieu's (1999 [1993]) introduction to *The Weight of the World*.

8 See my monographs on urban policing (Fassin 2013 [2011]) and the carceral condition (Fassin 2017a [2015]) in contemporary France.

9 See Axel Honneth (1995 [1992] and 2007 [2000]).

10 See David Owen's (2002) enlightening discussion.

11 See my tentative defense and illustration of critique (Fassin 2017b).

References

Abélès, Marc (2010 [2006]), *The Politics of Survival*, trans. Julie Kleinman, Durham, NC: Duke University Press.

Abensour, Miguel (1982), "Le choix du petit," *Passé présent* 1: 59–72.

Abu-Lughod, Lila (1986), *Veiled Sentiments: Honor and Poetry in a Bedouin Society*, Berkeley, CA: University of California Press.

Adorno, Theodor (1974 [1951]), *Minima Moralia: Reflections on a Damaged Life*, trans. E. F. N. Jephcott, London: Verso.

Agamben, Giorgio (1998 [1995]), *Homo Sacer: Sovereign Power and Bare Life*, trans. Daniel Heller-Roazen, Stanford, CA: Stanford University Press.

Agamben, Giorgio (2000 [1996]), *Means Without End*, trans. Vincenzo Binetti and Cesare Casarino, Minneapolis, MN: University of Minnesota Press.

Agamben, Giorgio (2009 [2008]), *The Signature of All Things: On Method*, trans. Luca D'Isanto and Kevin Attell, New York: Zone Books.

Agamben, Giorgio (2013 [2011]), *The Highest Poverty: Monastic Rules and Form-of-Life*, trans. Adam Kotsko, Stanford, CA: Stanford University Press, pp. 3–4.

Agamben, Giorgio (2016 [2014]), *The Use of Bodies*, trans. Adam Kotsko, Stanford, CA: Stanford University Press, pp. 207–8.

Alexander, Michelle (2010), *The New Jim Crow: Mass Incarceration in the Age of Colorblindness*, New York: The New Press.

Allen, Lori (2013), *The Rise and Fall of Human Rights: Cynicism and Politics in Occupied Palestine*, Stanford, CA: Stanford University Press.

Anidjar, Gil (2011), "The Meaning of Life," *Critical Inquiry* 37/4: 697–723.

Antelme, Robert (1957 [1947]), *L'Espèce humaine*, Paris: Gallimard.

Arendt, Hannah (1990 [1963]), *On Revolution*, London: Penguin Books.

Arendt, Hannah (1996 [1943]), "We Refugees," in *Altogether Elsewhere: Writers in Exile*, Marc Robinson (eds.), Boston, MA: Faber and Faber, pp. 110–19.

Arendt, Hannah (1998 [1958]), *The Human Condition*, Chicago, IL: The University of Chicago Press.

Asad, Talal (1993), *Genealogies of Religion: Discipline and Reasons of Power in Christianity and Islam*, Baltimore, MD: Johns Hopkins University Press.

Asad, Talal (2007), *On Suicide Bombing*, New York: Columbia University Press.

Auden, W. H. (2011 [1947]), *The Age of Anxiety: A Baroque Eclogue*, Princeton, NJ: Princeton University Press.

Bargu, Banu (2014), *Starve and Immolate: The Politics of Human Weapons*, New York: Columbia University Press.

Bauman, Zygmunt (2007), *Consuming Life*, Cambridge: Polity.

Beckett, Samuel (1954 [1952]), *Waiting for Godot*, New York: Grove Press.

Beckett, Samuel (1955), *Molloy*, Paris: Olympia Press.

Benjamin, Walter (1968 [1942]), "Theses on the Philosophy of History," in *Illuminations: Essays and Reflections*, Hannah Arendt (ed.), New York: Schocken Books, pp. 253–64.

Benjamin, Walter (1986 [1920]), "Critique of Violence," trans. Edmund Jephcott, in *Reflections: Essays, Aphorisms, Autobiographical Writings*, Peter Demetz (ed.), New York: Schocken Books, pp. 277–300.

Bessire, Lucas (2014), *Behold the Black Caiman: A Chronicle of Ayoreo Life*, Chicago, IL: University of Chicago Press.

Biehl, João (2005), *Vita: Life in a Zone of Social Abandonment*, Berkeley, CA: University of California Press.

Biehl, João and Petryna, Adriana (eds.) (2013), *When People Come First, Critical Studies in Global Health*, Princeton, NJ: Princeton University Press.

Bourdieu, Pierre (1987 [1986]), "The Biographical Illusion," trans. Yves Winkin and Wendy Leeds-Hurwitz, *Working Papers of the Center for Psychosocial Studies* 14.

Bourdieu, Pierre (1999 [1993]), "The Space of Points of View," in *The Weight of the World: Social Suffering in Contemporary Society*, trans. Priscilla Parkhurst Ferguson, Cambridge: Polity, pp. 3–5.

Bradol, Jean-Hervé (2004 [2003]), "The Sacrificial International Order and Humanitarian Action," in Fabrice Weissman (ed.), *In the Shadow of 'Just Wars': Violence, Politics and Humanitarian Action*, Ithaca, NY: Cornell University Press, pp. 1–22.

Butler, Judith (2004), *Precarious Life: The Powers of Mourning and Violence*, London: Verso.

Canguilhem, Georges (1990), "Vie," *Encyclopædia Universalis*, corpus 23, Paris: Encyclopædia Universalis.

Canguilhem, Georges (1991 [1966]), *On The Normal and the Pathological*, trans. Carolyn Fawcett and Robert Cohen, New York: Zone Books.

Canguilhem, Georges (1994 [1968]), "La nouvelle connaissance de la vie," in *Études d'histoire et de philosophie des sciences concernant les vivants et la vie*, Paris: Vrin, pp. 335–64.

Canguilhem, Georges (2008 [1952]), *Knowledge of Life*, trans. Stefanos Geroulanos and Daniela Ginsburg, New York: Fordham University Press, pp. xvii–xviii.

Cavell, Stanley (1962), "The Availability of Wittgenstein's Later Philosophy," *The Philosophical Review* 71/1: 67–93.

Cavell, Stanley (1989), *This New Yet Unapproachable America: Lectures after Emerson after Wittgenstein*, Chicago, IL: The University of Chicago Press.

Chetty, Raj et al. (2016), "The Association Between Income and Life Expectancy in the United States, 2001–2014," *JAMA* 315/16: 1750–66.

Coates, Ta-Nehisi, (2015), *Between the World and Me*, New York: Penguin Books.

Coleman, William (1982), *Death is a Social Disease: Public Health and Political Economy in Early Industrial France*, Madison, WI: University of Wisconsin Press.

Darwish, Mahmoud (2009), *Almond Blossoms and Beyond*, trans. Mohammad Shaheen, Northampton: Interlink Publishing.

Das, Veena (2006), *Life and Words: Violence and the Descent into the Ordinary*, Berkeley, CA: University of California Press.

Das, Veena and Han, Clara (eds.) (2016), *Living and Dying in the Contemporary World: A Compendium*, Berkeley, CA: University of California Press.

Daston, Lorraine (1995), "The Moral Economy of Science," *Osiris* 10: 2–24.

Daston, Lorraine (2008), "Life, Chance & Life Chances," *Daedalus*, 137/1: 5–14.

Derrida, Jacques (2007 [2004]), *Learning to Live Finally: The Last Interview* (with Jean Birnbaum), trans. Pascale-Anne Brault and Michael Naas, Brooklyn, NY: Melville House.

Desmond, Matthew (2016), *Evicted: Poverty and Profit in the American City*, New York: Crown Publishers.

Dostoevsky, Fyodor (1992 [1864]), *Notes from the Underground*, trans. Constance Garnett, Mineola, NY: Dover Thrift Editions.

Duffield, Mark (2001), *Global Governance and the New Wars: The Merging of Development and Security*, London: Zed Books.

Durkheim, Émile (1974 [1906]), "The Determination of Moral Facts," in *Sociology and Philosophy*, trans. D. F. Pocock, Abingdon: Routledge, pp. 35–62.

Emmett, Kathleen (1990), "Forms of Life," *Philosophical Investigations* 13/3: 213–31.

Esposito, Roberto (2008 [2004]), *Bios: Biopolitics and Philosophy*, trans. Timothy Campbell, Minneapolis, MN: University of Minnesota Press, pp. 44–6.

Ewick, Patricia and Silbey, Susan (1998), *The Common Place of Law: Stories from Everyday Life*, Chicago, IL: University of Chicago Press.

Fassin, Didier (1991), "Handicaps physiques, pratiques économiques et stratégies matrimoniales au Sénégal," *Social Science & Medicine* 32/3: 267–72.

Fassin, Didier (1996), "Le gouvernement de la vie," in *L'Espace politique de la santé. Essai de généalogie*, Paris: PUF, pp. 199–281.

Fassin, Didier (2001), "Une double peine. La condition sociale des immigrés malades du sida," *L'Homme* 160: 137–62.

Fassin, Didier (2005), "Compassion and Repression: The Moral Economy of Immigration Policies in France," *Cultural Anthropology* 20/3: 362–87.

Fassin, Didier (2007a), "Humanitarianism as a Politics of Life," *Public Culture* 19/3: 499–520.

Fassin, Didier (2007b [2006]), *When Bodies Remember: Experiences and Politics of AIDS in South Africa*, trans. Amy Jacobs and Gabrielle Varro, Berkeley, CA: University of California Press.

Fassin, Didier (2008), "The Humanitarian Politics of Testimony: Subjectification through Trauma in the Israeli-Palestinian Conflict," *Cultural Anthropology* 23/3: 531–58.

Fassin, Didier (2009a), "Another Politics of Life is Possible," *Theory, Culture and Society* 26/5: 44–60.

Fassin, Didier (2009b), "A Violence of History: Accounting for AIDS in Post-apartheid South Africa," in Barbara Rylko-Bauer, Linda Whiteford, and Paul Farmer (eds.), *Global Health in Times of Violence*, Santa Fe, New Mexico: School of Advanced Research, pp. 113–35.

Fassin, Didier (2009c), "Moral Economies Revisited," *Annales. Histoire, sciences sociales* 64/6: 1237–66.

Fassin, Didier (2009d), *Inégalités et santé*, Paris: La Documentation française, Problèmes politiques et sociaux n°960.

Fassin, Didier (2010), "Ethics of Survival: A Democratic Approach to the Politics of Life," *Humanity* 1/1: 81–95.

Fassin, Didier (2011), *Humanitarian Reason: A Moral History of the Present*, trans. Rachel Gomme, Berkeley, CA: University of California Press.

Fassin, Didier (ed.) (2012), *Moral Anthropology: A Companion*, Malden, MA: Wiley-Blackwell.

Fassin, Didier (2013 [2011]), *Enforcing Order: An Ethnography of Urban Policing*, trans. Rachel Gomme, Cambridge: Polity.

Fassin, Didier (2014), "The Parallel Lives of Philosophy and Anthropology," in Veena Das, Michael Jackson, Arthur Kleinman, and Bhrigupati Singh (eds.), *The Ground Between: Anthropology Engages Philosophy*, Durham, NC: Duke University Press, pp. 50–70.

Fassin, Didier (2015a), "Économie morale de la protestation: De Ferguson à Clichy-sous-Bois, repenser les émeutes," *Mouvements* 83: 122–9.

Fassin, Didier (2015b), "Troubled Waters: At the Confluence of Ethics and Politics," in Michael Lambek, Veena Das, Didier Fassin, and Webb Keane (eds.), *Four Lectures on Ethics: Anthropological Perspectives*, Chicago, IL: Hau Books, pp. 175–210.

Fassin, Didier (2016), "The Value of Life and the Worth of Lives," in Veena Das and Clara Han (eds.), *Living and Dying in the Contemporary World: A Compendium*, Berkeley, CA: University of California Press, pp. 770–83.

Fassin, Didier (2017a [2015]), *Prison Worlds: An Ethnography of the Carceral Condition*, trans. Rachel Gomme, Cambridge: Polity.

Fassin, Didier (2017b), "The Endurance of Critique," *Anthropological Theory* 17/1: 4–29.

Fassin, Didier (2018 [2017c]), *The Will to Punish*, Oxford: Oxford University Press.

Fassin, Didier and Bourdelais, Patrice (eds.) (2005), *Les Constructions de l'intolérable: Études d'histoire et d'anthropologie sur les frontières de l'espace moral*, Paris: La Découverte.

Fassin, Didier and Eideliman, Jean-Sébastien (eds.) (2012), *Économies morales contemporaines*, Paris: La Découverte.

Fassin, Didier and Lézé, Samuel (2014), *Moral Anthropology: A Critical Reader*, London, New York: Routledge.

Fassin, Didier and Rechtman, Richard (2009 [2007]), *The Empire of Trauma: An Inquiry Into the Condition of Victimhood*, Princeton, NJ: Princeton University Press.

Fassin, Didier, Wilhelm-Solomon, Matthew, and Segatti, Aurelia (2017), "Asylum as a Form of Life: The Politics and Experience of Indeterminacy in South Africa," *Current Anthropology* 58/2: 160–87.

Faubion, James (2001), *The Shadows and Lights of Waco: Millenialism Today*, Princeton, NJ: Princeton University Press.

Fehér, Ferenc and Heller, Agnes (1994), *Biopolitics*, Aldershot: Ashgate.

Feinberg, Kenneth (2005), *What is Life Worth? The Unprecedented Effort to Compensate Victims of 9/11*, New York: Public Affairs.

Foucault, Michel (1978 [1976]), *The History of Sexuality, Volume 1: An Introduction*, trans. Robert Hurley, New York: Random House.

Foucault, Michel (1985 [1984]), *The History of Sexuality, Volume 2: The Use of Pleasure*, trans. Robert Hurley, New York: Random House.

Foucault, Michel (2003a [1985]), "Life: Experience and Science," in *The Essential Foucault*, ed. Paul Rabinow and Nikolas Rose, New York: The New Press, pp. 6–17.

Foucault, Michel (2003b [1997]), *Society Must Be Defended: Lectures at the Collège de France 1975–1976*, trans. David Macey, New York: Picador.

Foucault, Michel (2007 [2004]), *Security, Territory, Population, Lectures at the Collège de France 1977–1978*, trans. Graham Burchel, New York: Picador.

Foucault, Michel (2008 [2004]), *The Birth of Biopolitics: Lectures at the Collège de France 1978–1979*, trans. Graham Burchel, New York: Picador.

Frank, Gelya (1995), "Anthropology and Individual Lives: The Story of the Life History and the History of Life Stories," *American Anthropologist* 97/1: 145–8.

Franklin, Sarah and Lock, Margaret (eds.) (2003), *Remaking Life and Death: Toward an Anthropology of the Biosciences*, Santa Fe, New Mexico: School of American Research Press.

Fraser, Nancy and Honneth, Axel (2003), *Redistribution or Recognition? A Political-Philosophical Exchange*, trans. Joel Golb, James Ingram, and Christiane Wilke, London: Verso.

Fullwiley, Duana (2011), *The Enculturated Gene: Sickle Cell Health Politics and Biological Difference in West Africa*, Princeton, NJ: Princeton University Press.

Garces, Chris (2012), "The Cross Politics of Ecuador's Penal State," *Cultural Anthropology* 25/3: 459–96.

Goffman, Alice (2014), *On The Run: Fugitive Life in an American City*, Chicago, IL: University of Chicago Press.

Gottschalk, Marie (2015), *Caught: The Prison State and the Lockdown of American Politics*, Princeton, NJ: Princeton University Press.

Guenther, Lisa (2013), *Solitary Confinement: Social Deaths and Its Afterlives*, Minneapolis, MN: University of Minnesota Press.

Habermas, Jürgen (1990 [1985]), *The Philosophical Discourse of Modernity: Twelve Lectures*, trans. Frederick Lawrence, Cambridge, MA: MIT Press.

Hacking, Ian (1990), *The Taming of Chance*, Cambridge: Cambridge University Press.

Halbwachs, Maurice (1913), *La Théorie de l'homme moyen: Essai sur Quetelet et la statistique morale*, Paris: Alcan.

Hanna-Attisha, Mona, et al. (2016), "Elevated Blood Lead Levels in Children Associated with the Flint Drinking Water Crisis," *American Journal of Public Health* 106/2: 283–90.

Hartigan, John (2014), *Aesop's Anthropology: A Multispecies Approach*, Minneapolis, MN: University of Minnesota.

Hartman, Saidiya (2008), "Venus in Two Acts," *Small Axe* 12/2: 1–14.

Hegel, Georg Wilhelm Friedrich (1991 [1820]), *Elements of the Philosophy of Right*, trans. H. B. Nisbet, Cambridge: Cambridge University Press.

Helmreich, Stefan (1998), *Silicon Second Nature: Culturing Artificial Life in a Digital World*, Berkeley, CA: University of California Press.

Holmes, Seth (2013), *Fresh Fruit, Broken Bodies: Migrant Farmworkers in the United States*, Berkeley, CA: University of California Press.

Honneth, Axel (1995 [1992]), *The Struggle for Recognition: The Moral Grammar of Social Conflicts*, trans. Joel Anderson, Cambridge: Polity.

Honneth, Axel (2007 [2000]), *Disrespect: The Normative Foundations of Critical Theory*, Cambridge: Polity.

Horkheimer, Max (1972 [1968]), *Critical Theory: Selected Essays*, New York: Seabury Press.

Howell, Signe (ed.) (1997), *The Ethnography of Moralities*, London: Routledge.

Hughes, Everett (1962), "Good People and Dirty Work," *Social Problems* 10/1: 3–11.

Ingold, Tim (2010), "Footprints through the Weather-world: Walking, Breathing, Knowing," *Journal of the Royal Anthropological Institute* 16/1: S121–S139.

Ingold, Tim (2011), *Being Alive: Essays on Movement, Knowledge and Description*, London: Routledge.

Inhorn, Marcia and Wentzell, Emily (eds.) (2012), *Medical Anthropology at the Intersections: Histories, Activisms, and Futures*, Durham, NC: Duke University Press.

Jackson, Michael (2011), *Life Within Limits: Well-Being in a World of Want*, Durham, NC: Duke University Press.

Jaeggi, Rahel (2005), " 'No Individual Can Resist': *Minima Moralia* as Critique of Forms of Life," *Constellations* 12/1: 65–82.

Kazanjian, David (2016), "Two Paths through Slavery's Archives," *History of the Present* 6/2: 133–45.

Keenleyside, Heather (2012), "The First-Person Form of Life: Locke, Sterne, and the Autobiographical Animal," *Critical Inquiry* 39: 116–41.

Khurana, Thomas (2013), "The Freedom of Life: An Introduction," in *The Freedom of Life: Hegelian Perspectives*, Thomas Khurana (ed.), Cologne: August Verlag Berlin, pp. 11–32.

King, Matthew (2009), "Clarifying the Foucault-Habermas Debate: Morality, Ethics, and 'Normative Foundations'," *Philosophy and Social Criticism* 35/3: 287–314.

Kohn, Eduardo (2007), "How Dogs Dream: Amazonian Natures and the Politics of Transspecies Engagement," *American Ethnologist* 34/1: 3–24.

Kohn, Eduardo (2013), *How Forests Think: Toward an Anthropology Beyond the Human*, Berkeley, CA: University of California Press.

Koselleck, Reinhart (2004 [1979]), *On the Semantic of Historical Time*, trans. Keith Tribe, New York: Columbia University Press.

Krieger, Nancy (2000), "Discrimination and Health," in Lisa Berkman and Ichiro Kawachi (eds.), *Social Epidemiology*, Oxford: Oxford University Press, pp. 36–75.

Laidlaw, James (1995), *Riches and Renunciation: Religion, Economy and Society Among the Jains*, Oxford: Clarendon Press.

Laidlaw, James (2014), *The Subject of Virtue: An Anthropology of Ethics and Freedom*, Cambridge: Cambridge University Press.

Lambek, Michael (2015), *The Ethical Condition: Essays on Action, Person and Value*, Chicago, IL: University of Chicago Press.

Laugier, Sandra (2015), "La vulnérabilité des formes de vie," *Raisons politiques* 57: 65–80.

Lear, Jonathan (1986), "Transcendental Anthropology," in Philip Pettit and John McDowell (eds.), *Subject, Context and Thought*, Oxford: Clarendon Press, pp. 267–98.

Lebovic, Nitzan (2006), "The Beauty and Terror of *Lebensphilosophie*: Ludwig Klages, Walter Benjamin, and Alfred Baeumler," *South Central Review* 23/1: 23–39.

Leclerc, Annette (ed.) et al. (2000), *Les Inégalités sociales de santé*, Paris: La Découverte.

Lefort, Claude (1991 [1981]), "Permanence of the Theologico-Political?," in *Democracy and Political Theory*, Cambridge: Polity, pp. 213–55.

Leibbrandt, Murray, Poswell, Laura, Naidoo, Pranushka, and Welch, Matthew (2006), "Measuring Recent Changes in South African Inequality and Poverty," in Haroon Bhorat and Ravi Kanbur (eds.), *Poverty and Policy in Post-Apartheid South Africa*, Pretoria: HSRC Press, pp. 95–142.

Lemke, Thomas (2011), *Biopolitics: An Advanced Introduction*, New York: New York University Press.

Lévinas, Emmanuel (1979 [1961]), *Totality and Infinity: An Essay on Interiority*, trans. Alphonso Lingis, Dordrecht: Kluwer Academic Publishers.

Lévi-Strauss, Claude (1969 [1949]), *The Elementary Structures of Kinship*, trans. James Harle Bell, John Richard von Sturmer, and Rodney Needham, Boston, MA: Beacon Press.

Lewis, Oscar (1961), *The Children of Sánchez: Autobiography of a Mexican Family*, New York: Vintage.

Lewis, Philip (1985), "The Measure of Translation Effects," in *Difference in Translation*, Joseph Graham (ed.), Ithaca, NY: Cornell University Press, pp. 31–62.

Locke, John (1836 [1689]), *An Essay Concerning Human Understanding*. London: T. Tegg & Son.

Lovell, Anne, Stefania Pandolfo, Veena Das, and Sandra Laugier (2013), *Face aux désastres: Une conversation à quatre voix sur la folie, le care et les grandes détresses collectives*, Montreuil: Ithaque.

Macé, Marielle (2016), *Styles: Critique de nos formes de vie*, Paris: Gallimard.

Mahmood, Saba (2005), *The Politics of Piety: The Islamic Revival and the Feminist Subject*, Princeton, NJ: Princeton University Press.

Marrus, Michael (2002), *The Unwanted: European Refugees from the First World War through the Cold War*, Philadelphia, PA: Temple University Press.

Massey, Douglas (2007), *Categorically Unequal: The American Stratification System*, New York: Russell Sage Foundation.

Meillassoux, Claude (1986), *Anthropologie de l'esclavage: Le ventre de fer et d'acier*, Paris: PUF.

Musil, Robert (1995 [1930]), *The Man Without Qualities*, trans. Sophie Wilkins and Burton Pike, London: Picador.

Nehamas, Alexander (1998), *The Art of Living: Socratic Reflections from Plato to Foucault*, Berkeley, CA: University of California Press.

Nietzsche, Friedrich (1989 [1887]), *On the Genealogy of Morals*, trans. Walter Kaufman, New York: Vintage Books.

Nietzsche, Friedrich (2001 [1882]), *The Gay Science: With a Prelude in German Rhymes and an Appendix of Songs*, trans. Josefine Nauckhoff, Cambridge: Cambridge University Press.

Ogien, Albert (2015), "La démocratie comme revendication et forme de vie," *Raisons politiques* 57: 31–47.

Olshansky, Jay et al. (2012), "Differences in Life Expectancy Due to Race and Educational Differences Are Widening and Many May Not Catch Up," *Health Affairs* 31/18: 1803–10.

Owen, David (2002), "Criticism and Captivity: On Genealogy and Critical Theory," *European Journal of Philosophy* 10/2: 216–30.

Parrenas, Rhacel (2001), *Servants of Globalization: Migration and Domestic Work*, Stanford, CA: Stanford University Press.

Patterson, Orlando (1982), *Slavery and Social Death: A Comparative Study*, Cambridge, MA: Harvard University Press.

Perec, Georges (1987 [1978]), *Life: A User's Manual*, trans. David Bellos, London: Collins Harvill.

Peters, Rudolph (2006), *Crime and Punishment in Islamic Law: Theory and Practice from the Sixteenth to the Twenty-first Century*, Cambridge: Cambridge University Press.

Petryna, Adriana (2002), *Life Exposed: Biological Citizens after Chernobyl*, Princeton, NJ: Princeton University Press.

Pitrou, Perig (2014), "La vie, un objet pour l'anthropologie ? Options méthodologiques et problèmes épistémologiques," *L'Homme* 212: 159–89.

Porter, Theodore (1988), *The Rise of Statistical Thinking, 1820–1900*, Princeton, NJ: Princeton University Press.

Proust, Marcel (1996 [1927]), *In Search of Lost Time*, vol. 6: *Time Regained*, trans. Andreas Mayor and Terence Kilmartin, London: Vintage.

Rabinow, Paul (1999), *French DNA: Trouble in Purgatory*. Chicago, IL: University of Chicago Press.

Rabinow, Paul and Caduff, Carlo (2006), "Life – After Canguilhem," *Theory, Culture & Society* 23/2–3: 329–31.

Rabinow, Paul and Rose, Nikolas (2006), "Biopower today," *BioSocieties* 1/1: 195–217.

Ralph, Laurence (2014), *Renegade Dreams: Living Through Injury in Gangland Chicago*, Chicago, IL: University of Chicago Press.

Read, Kenneth (1955), "Morality and the Concept of the Person among the Gahuku-Gama," *Oceania* 25/4: 233–82.

Rimbaud, Arthur (2004 [1873]), *A Season in Hell*, trans. Jeremy Denbow, Lincoln: iUniverse.

Rios, Victor (2011), *Punished: Policing the Lives of Black and Latino Boys*, New York: New York University Press.

Robbins, Joel (2004), *Becoming Sinners: Christianity and Moral Torment in a Papua New Guinea Society*, Berkeley, CA: University of California Press.

Rose, Nikolas (2007), *The Politics of Life Itself: Biomedicine, Power, and Subjectivity in the Twenty-First Century*, Princeton, NJ: Princeton University Press.

Rousseau, Jean-Jacques (1985 [1754]), *A Discourse on Inequality*, New York: Penguin Books.

Rudder Baker, Lynne (2008), "On the Very Idea of a Form of Life," *Inquiry: An Interdisciplinary Journal of Philosophy* 27/1–4: 277–89.

Schelling, Thomas (1984), "The Life You Save May Be Your Own," in *Choice and Consequence*, Cambridge, MA: Harvard University Press, pp. 113–46.

Scheper-Hughes, Nancy (1992), *Death Without Weeping: The Violence of Everyday Life in Brazil*, Berkeley, CA: University of California Press.

Schlanger, Margo (2013), "Prison Segregation: Symposium Introduction and Preliminary Data on Racial Disparities," *Michigan Journal of Race & Law* 18: 241–50.

Schneider, Cathy Lisa (2014), *Police Power and Race Riots: Violent Unrest in Paris and New York*, Philadelphia, PA: University of Pennsylvania Press.

Schor, Ralph (1996), *Histoire de l'immigration en France de la fin du XIXe siècle à nos jours*, Paris: Armand Colin.

Schrödinger, Erwin (1944), *What is Life? The Physical Aspect of the Living Cell*, Cambridge: Cambridge University Press.

Schultz, Theodore (ed.) (1974), *Economics of the Family: Marriage, Children, and Human Capital*, Chicago, IL: University of Chicago Press.

Seager, Sara et al. (2016), "Toward a List of Molecules as Potential Biosignature Gases for the Search of Life on Exoplanets and Applications to Terrestrial Biochemistry," *Astrobiology* 16/6: 465–85.

Simmel, Georg (1978 [1907]), *The Philosophy of Money*, trans. Tom Bottomore and David Frisby, London: Routledge & Kegan Paul.

Singer, Peter (2009), *The Life You Can Save: Acting Now to End World Poverty*, New York: Random House.

Singh, Bhrigupati (2015), *Poverty and the Quest for Life: Spiritual and Material Striving in Rural India*, Chicago, IL: University of Chicago Press.

Steiner, George (1975), "The Hermeneutic Motion," in *After Babel: Aspects of Language and Translation*, Oxford: Oxford University Press, pp. 296–303.

Stevenson, Lisa (2014), *Life Besides Itself: Imagining Care in the Canadian Arctic*, Berkeley, CA: University of California Press.

Surak, Kristin (2013), "Guestworkers: A Taxonomy," *The New Left Review* 84: 84–102.

Thomas, William and Znaniecki, Florian (1996 [1920]), *The Polish Peasant in Europe and America: A Classic Work in Immigration History*, Urbana/Chicago, IL: University of Illinois Press.

Thompson, E. P. (1971), "The Moral Economy of the English Crowd in the Eighteenth Century," *Past & Present* 50: 76–136.

Torpey, John (1986), "Ethics and Critical Theory: From Horkheimer to Habermas," *Telos. Critical Theory of the Contemporary* 69: 68–84.

Vailly, Joëlle, Kehr, Janina, and Niewöhner, Jörg (eds.) (2011), *De la vie biologique à la vie sociale: Approches sociologiques et anthropologiques*, Paris: La Découverte.

Weber, Max (1994 [1919]), "Politics as a Vocation," in Peter Lassman and Ronald Speirs (eds.), *Weber: Political Writings*, trans. Ronald Speirs, Cambridge: Cambridge University Press, pp. 309–69.

Weiss, Madeline, et al. (2016), "The Physiology and Habitat of the Last Universal Common Ancestor," *Nature Microbiology* 1 (July 25), available at: <doi:10.1038/nmicrobiol.2016.116>.

Westermarck, Edward (1906), *The Origin and Development of Moral Ideas*, 2 vols, London: Macmillan.

Western, Bruce (2006), *Punishment and Inequality in America*, New York: Russell Sage Foundation.

Williams, Bernard (1974), "Wittgenstein and Idealism," in *Understanding Wittgenstein*, Royal Institute of Philosophy Lectures, London: Macmillan, pp. 76–95.

Williams, David, et al. (2010), "Race, Socioeconomic Status and Health," *Annals of the New York Academy of Sciences* 1186: 69–101.

Wittgenstein, Ludwig (1998 [1977]), *Culture and Value: A Selection from the Posthumous Remains*, ed. Henrik von Wright, Georg and Nyman Heikki, Oxford: Blackwell Publishers.

Wittgenstein, Ludwig (2009 [1953]), *Philosophical Investigations*, trans. G. E. M. Anscombe, revised by P. M. S. Hacker and Joachim Schulte, Malden, MA: Wiley-Blackwell.

Wool, Zoë (2015), *After War: The Weight of Life at Walter Reid*, Durham, NC: Duke University Press.

Zelizer, Viviana (2011), *Economic Lives: How Culture Shapes the Economy*, Princeton, NJ: Princeton University Press.

Zigon, Jarrett (2011), *"HIV is God's Blessing," Rehabilitating Morality in Neoliberal Russia*, Berkeley, CA: University of California Press.

Index